Organizational Consulting

Also by Alan Weiss

Organizational Consulting

How to Be an Effective Internal Change Agent

Alan Weiss, PhD

John Wiley & Sons, Inc.

Library of Congress Cataloging-in-Publication Data:

Weiss, Alan, 1946–
   Organizational consulting : how to be an effective internal change agent / Alan Weiss.
      p. cm.
   Includes bibliographical references and index.
   ISBN 0-471-26378-8 (cloth : alk. paper)
   1. Business consultants. 2. Organizational change. 3. Organizational effectiveness. I. Title.
HD69.C6 W462 2003
001'.068—dc21   2002026743

Printed in the United States of America.

10 9 8 7 6 5 4 3 2 1

This is for all human resources people who have opposed silly management policies, exposed illegal and unethical conduct, and who are unafraid to speak their minds—corporate politics and powerful executives notwithstanding. In other words, it's for those who have fought the good fight. You know who you are.

Acknowledgments

My thanks to my editor at Wiley, Michael Hamilton, who makes it so easy that I should be paying him. Unfortunately for him, this acknowledgment will have to suffice.

Contents

Introduction

This is the first book I've written (of more than 20) focused solely on internal consulting. There are two reasons for that. First, the publisher asked me to do it. Second, as an independent consultant, I've often competed against internal resources for projects, and I figured "Why provide help to the competition?" In actuality, I've worked hand-in-glove with a great many exceptional human resources professionals, trainers, internal consultants, and other organizational change agents over the years. They are some of the best colleagues I've had, and I've learned more from them than they've learned from me. So perhaps the third and best reason for this book is actually payback.

What I often hear from internal people when I'm hired by an executive is, "Thank goodness you're here. You'll tell them the same things we've been saying for years, but at your rate of pay, they'll listen to you!" Unfortunately for the organization, that's been all too true.

My intent in this book is to demonstrate that internal consulting is more similar to external consulting than it is dissimilar. But the inherent advantages of being a part of the culture are often sacrificed in the name of the fad-of-the-month, the latest guru, and other dalliances into worlds strange and far away—and not of the least interest to line executives (and not of the least relevance).

As I write this I've just read a book review of something called *Guiding Change Journeys*, largely panned by *Training* magazine. It includes advice on getting senior managers to sit together, close their eyes, and meditate; there are "archetypal change journeys"; "karmic loops"; and "dragon charts." There is simply too much of this stuff circulating in the human resources community. It's laughable to the rest of us, but it's killing internal change agents.

One final word: I offer here the best of my advice gained over 25 years consulting to Fortune 1,000 organizations of every type. I don't claim it's the royal road, only one road. I've made mistakes and so will you, and every consulting project has rough edges and setbacks. There is no such thing as a flawless consultant or perfect consulting, at least not in this world. *Our lives are about success, not perfection.* I've chosen to reference my own works where relevant in the footnotes, but every chapter will conclude with suggested reading by another author whose work I deem appropriate, supportive, and enriching for the subjects discussed (with the rare exception of when one of my books has no peer on that subject). Think of them as the wine selections the captain offers with your meal.

The only things that matter are results. I'm confident that you can improve your ability to generate dramatic results immediately if you simply utilize the techniques in this book that appeal to you and apply to your environment. In that case, we've both done our jobs.

—Alan Weiss, Ph.D.
East Greenwich, RI

October 2002

Organizational Consulting

PART ONE

THE ENVIRONMENT

If It Walks Like a Duck

What Constitutes an Effective Internal Consultant?

THE ROLE OF A CONSULTANT

I'm going to be talking about consultants. It doesn't matter what your title is. The topic includes human resources professionals, trainers, facilitators, change agents, and whatever else may be on your business card.

A consultant is someone who provides expertise for a client for a particular issue, concern, opportunity, or problem. That expertise may include knowledge, experiences, processes, models, behaviors, technology, or other assets. An external and internal consultant both provide this expertise in return for remuneration for the value provided. For an external consultant, that remuneration is usually a fee. For an internal consultant, that remuneration is usually a job (and the continuance thereof).

The consultant has a basic, overarching role, which guides all subordinate roles: That role is to improve the client's condition.

Just as the doctors say, "First, do no harm," the consultant is only successful if the client is better off after the engagement than before. That improvement may be in the form of a problem fixed, an opportunity exploited, a disaster averted, confidence validated, or any number of other salutary results. But if you haven't improved the client's condition, then you haven't been successful.

This means that our roles are those of advisors. We don't do the work, per se. When a consultant becomes the temporary (or de facto) director of sales, he or she is no longer a consultant but an employee filling a key position. It's up to our client to assess our advice and make appropriate decisions. After all, if the lawyers made the legal decisions, the auditors the financial decisions, and the consultants the management decisions, then why would we need managers?

> Consultants are basically advisors to management who must provide objective, pragmatic, and honest advice to their clients. If there is a trusting relationship, then the clients will always be confident that their best interests are being served, no matter how threatening, contrarian, or painful that advice may be.

Consulting is a relationship business. That means we must develop trusting relationships with internal partners and clients. To me, trust means that *both parties have the underlying conviction that the other person has the partner's absolute best interests in mind.* If I believe that about you, then I'm much more likely to listen to unprecedented, painful, and/or counterintuitive advice. I'll give you the benefit of the doubt (as you will extend that to me).

One of the key problems in internal consulting is a lack of trust. We address this as we progress, but we all know that a lack of credibility attached to a department or function also attaches itself to individuals representing that department or function. When that's the case, it's far easier to build individual trust and credibility than it is to change an entire department's reputation. When enough individuals have made the change, the department will benefit. But functions do not change perceptions; people do. Departments don't earn trust; individuals do.

The role of an internal consultant should place an emphasis on anticipation, improvement, and innovation. There has been an inordi-

---

Ten Ways to Develop, Nurture, and/or Recover Trust with Line Partners

1. Learn their issues and understand the realities of their business objectives.
2. Don't approach with a boxed solution, but listen and customize your response.
3. Overcommunicate, and be proactive in your communications.
4. Seek personal interactions over e-mail and voice messages.
5. Proactively suggest approaches to improve their operation; don't wait for pain.
6. Eschew all jargon; "left brain/right brain" thinkers, or "driver expressives" really don't matter.
7. Use only validated tools and bury the fads. There aren't many people today using "open meetings" or "future search," or any other nonsense that has no valid base.
8. Spend time doing the work. Don't spend a career in HR or training; work in sales, service, information technology (IT), finance, or wherever you can make a contribution and learn the business.
9. Use metrics that demonstrate progress directly related to your intervention.
10. Share credit, but also take credit. Develop a network of supporters, testimonials, and a history of success.

---

nate concentration on problem solving. While always important, problem solving has become a fairly mechanized routine and therefore of less value, despite its frequency. Problem solving basically restores performance to past levels.

But innovation raises the bar and is of much higher value. Since most managers have their noses pressed tightly to the glass of their own operations, they often fail to see the opportunity surrounding them. Catching up with the competition is important, but creating a gap between yourself and the next closest competitor is invaluable.

As a rule, internal consultants have been far too reactive and not nearly proactive enough. Figure 1.1 illustrates the difference between problem solving and innovation.

Finally, an important part of the role is to disagree. We're often swept along in the fervor of an executive's bright idea, but no one has had the fortitude to point out that no one is wearing any clothes. Outstanding (and trustworthy) consultants push back. They consider legality, ethics, pragmatics, risks, and costs to other parties. They don't blindly implement.

We have an excellent plumber. He arrives on time, fixes the leaks, and charges according to his efforts. But we would never ask him to come in and discuss the way the kitchen is decorated or the location of the bathrooms.

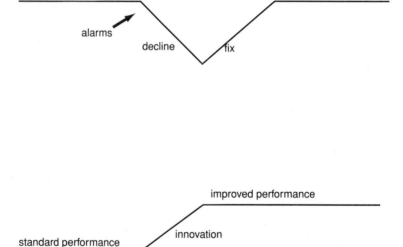

FIGURE 1.1 Problem solving vs. innovation

You must dedicate time to investigate how you can improve the operations of unsuspecting potential clients. Problems call out to you, but opportunity hides around the bend. Help your clients to recognize the bonanza awaiting, and formulate plans to exploit it. Don't be a firefighter—be a prospector.

We need plumbers to fix the leaks. But I don't think anyone reading this sees his or her future mending the corporate pipes.

THE KEY PLAYERS

The most important person in the consultant's universe is the *economic buyer*. The economic buyer is that person who can actually pay for your services. If there's a charge back system, then the economic buyer's budget is the one charged. In any case, he or she is the one whose project is involved.

Other hallmarks of the economic buyer:

✔ They specify the results that are required.
✔ They can allocate resources.
✔ They are the clearly perceived sponsor or champion.
✔ They will evaluate results.
✔ Their unit or function is the target of the improved condition.
✔ They are taking the risk and reaping the rewards.
✔ The buck stops there.

The economic buyer, in effect, writes the check. There is not a direct hierarchical corollary. Division managers and department heads are often economic buyers (as are always CEOs, CFOs, etc.), but the critical element is the ability to fund the project without further approval. My key buyer in Merck for years was a man with the title of manager of international development, and in Hewlett-Packard a woman who held the position of director of knowledge management.

Many internal consultants try to avoid the economic buyer. Often intimidating and usually influential, the economic buyer presents a problem in some cases, especially in an organization setting in which you've each had your roles defined for a long time. You may well have separate colleagues, never attend the same meetings, and even eat lunch in different settings.

> The economic buyer is the person with whom you must partner. If you settle for the buyer's subordinates, you likely become an implementer and not a consultant.

No matter. As a consultant, you need to be a partner of the buyer for the project. If you treat the buyer with deference due the position, or imbue him with Gnostic wisdom because of his rank, or refuse to oppose her because of fear of retribution, then you're a sycophant, not a consultant.

Most projects also have *critical sponsors*. These are people whose

---

Case Study

I was working with Mercedes-Benz North America, and the entire staff was scared to death of the president, a haughty and tough German national. He intimidated the heck out of everyone, and otherwise strong people became obsequious fawners in his presence.

One day he asked if I would do something and I told him I couldn't because it was a bad idea. I explained how the dealers would instantly dislike it, and that it would reflect poorly on him without any commensurate gain.

"You're absolutely right," he quickly concluded, and then added, "Why can't my own people point that out? Not one of them opposed this, and you made it instantly clear that it's a horrid idea. Why do we need to bring in outsiders to tell me the truth?"

Why, indeed?

support can enlist others to the cause but whose opposition—even quietly—can undermine the entire endeavor. A critical sponsor may be:

- ✔ An influential direct report of the buyer.
- ✔ A union officer.
- ✔ A highly successful salesperson.
- ✔ A major customer.
- ✔ An informal, respected leader.

It's important to co-opt the critical sponsors. That means that you and the buyer (hence, one more reason for a trusting partnership there) devise a strategy to convert key sponsors to the cause. This may be an appeal by the buyer, an appeal by you, careful relationship building, the identification of their self-interests, and so on. It may be different for each sponsor. The important thing is to bring them aboard before they scuttle the boat.

Implementers are those people who will have a responsibility for executing the appropriate actions and/or adopting the required behaviors. They may well be resistant, since the present is usually comfortable and the future is problematic. But they must be made situationally uncomfortable, so that maintaining the status quo is not possible.

It's not important that implementers like you; it's simply important that they change in the manner desired. A sales team might not like cross-selling several products when it was accustomed to specializing in a single product, but that's the direction in which they must be driven. The ideal agents for persuading implementers, in order of quality, are:

1. Appeal to enlightened self-interest. Persuade the implementer that he or she is better off by indulging in the new behaviors. For example, demonstrate a higher potential income, or more latitude of action, or greater learning potential.

2. Peer pressure. Develop a sufficient critical mass of converts so that any holdouts seem unenlightened and left in the dust. (The psychologists call this "normative pressure.") If enough people seem happy to make the changes requested, a momentum will be created that will affect the onlookers.

3. Coercion. Make it unbearably painful to continue to resist. The buyer might use the financial pressure inherent in evaluations, incentive compensation, and bonuses; job assignments might be increasingly unpleasant; status may be reduced; there can even be threats about retaining one's position. This is a tactic solely within the purview of the buyer, since the consultant wields no such power.

Move the implementers by whatever means necessary, but *move them*.

Finally, there are *stakeholders* of various types and varying degrees. These are people whose work or results will be impacted by the project. They may be employees, customers, vendors, management, shareholders, and so on. They have some stake in the quality of the outcomes.

> Key sponsors will, in turn, greatly influence implementers and stakeholders, so it's a good idea to identify each such sponsor and develop a strategy with the economic buyer as to how to best persuade each one to back your project.

It's a good idea to sample stakeholders early to determine their perceptions of their roles, interests, and impact in terms of the success of the project. It's crazy, for example, to introduce a new incentive system without sampling the sales force or a new pricing policy without talking to customers.

The ideal project will include a partnering relationship with the economic buyer; a strategy that successfully persuades all key sponsors to back you; focused and relatively rapid movement of implementers to execute the plan; and stakeholders who can recognize and support their own improved conditions due to the project.

Having said all that, if you don't have a relationship with the economic buyer, the odds are stacked greatly against you.

THE BASIC DYNAMICS

There are interpersonal and cultural dynamics that occur in virtually every consulting project. Four of these constants are important to master:

1. Resistance to change.
2. Process versus content.
3. The role of culture.
4. We've heard every objection.

1. Resistance to change.

There is a generally accepted myth that holds that people resist change. I've found that to be totally untrue. Every day, people adapt to, adjust for, and anticipate change in the form of roads closed, surprises from their family (good or bad), organizational shifting of priorities, cancellations, abrupt requests, and so on. If people were reluctant to change, we'd all be on heavy medication. Change is the universal norm, and it is both omnipresent and accepted.

What people do resist, however, is ambiguity. Some changes do not involve ambiguity, such as a highway detour that puts one on familiar, though less-traveled streets, or a work shift that involves a sudden trip, but to a site often visited. Other changes produce significant ambiguities: a road detour that takes one to completely unfamiliar territory or a sudden trip to a new country, new client, or new problem.

> People do not generally resist change, per se. They do resist venturing into unfamiliar and potentially harmful territory. It's up to the consultant to provide maps, lighting, and warm clothing.

In organizational change work, most people can relate to the picture painted of the future organization, and all people are intimately familiar with where they are today. But the journey to that new future is likely to be highly ambiguous and unclear. William Bridges calls this

The Neutral Zone and I've called it The Ambiguous Zone.[1] The concept is illustrated in Figure 1.2.

Work with your client to establish *not only the future state desired, but also the details of the journey.* For example, delineate the details of the transition, the numbers of people affected, what the universe of stakeholders looks like, likely obstacles, and so on. You'll find that the implementers are far more comfortable following a game plan—and even deviating from it, if necessary—than proceeding with no game plan at all.

People don't resist change. They resist being thrust into the unknown. Or, as my son put it once when much younger, "I'm not afraid of the dark. I'm afraid of what might be *in* the dark."

2. *Process versus content.*

Almost everyone reading this is a *process* consultant. By that I mean that the work you do (in negotiating, facilitating, training, conflict resolution, retention, succession planning, strategy, career development, ad infinitum) is applicable over vast acres of the corporate

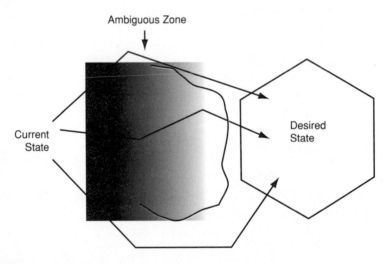

FIGURE 1.2 The Ambiguous Zone position

[1]See, for example, William Bridges' *Managing Transitions* (Addison Wesley, 1991) or my *Process Consulting* (Jossey-Bass/Pfeiffer, 2002).

Case Study

At one point I was assisting a call center response unit of Hewlett-Packard to switch to sophisticated new technology, with the intended result of reversing the prior ratio of 10 technical assistance calls answered electronically and 90 by a human being. With 90 percent of future calls responded to automatically, vast cost savings and increased customer efficiencies were projected.

However, we had to be careful to specify the steps that would be taken to reassign current staff; for job posting and bidding criteria; to provide skills and development for new assignments; and to specify clear time frames over which the transition would be finalized.

Our most important detail was to explain that the jobs remaining could not be assigned by lottery or seniority, since that final 10 percent of calls that could not be answered automatically would be, by definition, very tough issues requiring very deep knowledge of the systems involved.

This has always represented to me the human side of reengineering, which requires substantial consulting skills, and which can and should be done by internal people wherever possible.

landscape. Just as good external consultants can readily work cross-industrially and cross-culturally, good internal consultants can readily work cross-functionally and cross-culturally.

In other words, "You don't know our business" is never an applicable phrase!

When the CEO of Merck looked askance when I told him I knew virtually nothing about pharmaceuticals, I reminded him that we were sitting in the midst of more than 15,000 people who knew pharmaceuticals quite well. "Why do you need another pharmaceutical expert?" I asked. "I thought you needed someone to run focus groups on diversity."

Processes (such as the previous examples) are applicable in any environment with any content. While it's important to be *conversant* in the organization's content, it's not important to be expert in it.

Now here's the beauty of the internal consultant: At least you are living in the environment and, the longer you are there, presumably, the more you do become a content expert in the organization's work, to a greater degree than an outsider like me ever could. But don't be tripped up internally. Just because you've worked primarily for sales doesn't mean you can't work for finance, and merely because you've been working domestically doesn't mean you can't provide your expertise internationally.

Many internal consultants make the mistake of believing that they must become as expert as the people they are trying to help, and that's just crazy. Consultants who work with medical practices can not perform surgery, and jury consultants don't attempt to try cases themselves in court (because they can't). In fact, the very power that you bring is that of someone untainted by the content and able to bring the best practices from a diverse array of internal units and operations. Whatever you do, don't become the content expert for actuarial services, or call center response, or building security.

The more processes you master, and the more agility with which you can apply them, the more potential customers you gain.

3. *The role of culture.*

This is one of the greatest red herrings to land in the boat. If I can change culture from the outside, you can transmogrify it from the inside.

What is culture? I'll give you my quick definition, which has made more than one executive stop short.

Culture is simply that set of beliefs that governs behavior.

That's it. There are civic, organizational, school, neighborhood, family, and all kinds of cultures. Sometimes we move through several in the course of a day, adjusting our behaviors accordingly. (Did you ever hear the refrain, "Watch your tone—you're not at work now!")

My point is not to allow the dreaded cultural gambit to thwart, undo, or sabotage you. "It's just our culture in this department" really means that the current belief system leads to those behaviors, and not that the behaviors are ingrained from the middle of an obscure reptilian brain of 30 million years' development hidden deep in our cerebral cortex. My response is always, "Well, what do you say we change it tomorrow?"

Culture is changed when belief systems change, and belief systems change when *key exemplars establish a different set of beliefs through their behavior.* If you want to change behavior, culture notwithstanding, then change the beliefs of the most visible and respected exemplars.

> In organizational life, no one believes what they read or hear. They believe only what they *see.* If you want to change people's behavior, change the exemplars' behavior. To do that, influence their belief systems. And then, voilà, the culture has changed!

Don't feel handcuffed by "culture." Cultures change all the time (if you don't believe that, look at Continental Airlines before and after CEO Gordon Bethune), based on the actions of leaders. As a consultant, don't try to change behavior from the ground up. It usually doesn't work. Start at the top. That's why I stressed earlier the need to establish partnering relationships with the economic buyer.

4. We've heard every objection.

There is no objection you haven't heard, assuming you've been on the job for longer than 20 minutes. I'm serious. If you hear a new objection from a line customer as to why a project can't proceed, or why he can't support it, or why she can't live up to her original commitments that you haven't heard 100 times before, then you either haven't been listening, or have the memory capacity of a fish.[2]

It is absolutely negligent to be thrown by an objection from one

---

[2]One of my great statistics from psychology: It seems a fish forgets everything it knows every four seconds, which is why the same fish can keep getting caught under the same circumstances. Some consultants have fishlike attention spans. They are continually flummoxed by the same thing that flummoxed them yesterday. That's why they're green around the gills.

of your buyers, implementers, sponsors, or other stakeholders. You should be prepared to deal with the objections *overwhelmingly*.

For example, I'm often asked by a prospect something like this. "We like you, but would it be wise for us to use you when we could be hiring a larger firm with more resources?" My reply is rapid and to the point. "No, not wise at all, because here are 10 reasons why you're better off with me:

1. You're always dealing with the principal.
2. I'm far more responsive.
3. I'm not juggling dozens of clients and hundreds of requests.
4. And so on."[3]

Here are typical client objections, pre- and post-implementation, which you'd better be able to handle immediately and forcefully. How many are you comfortable spontaneously rebutting?

✔ We don't have the time.
✔ The operation can't absorb the disruption right now.
✔ HR (or whoever) doesn't have credibility with the sales force (or whomever).
✔ I can't afford the resource commitment.
✔ We don't have the money.
✔ The clients will hate it.
✔ We tried it before and it didn't work.
✔ I won't proceed unless you give me some guarantees.
✔ You don't have the expertise to do this internally.
✔ In retrospect, I promised too much support and have to withdraw.
✔ We need to delay this for a while due to other priorities.

---

[3] I also have 10 reasons why a buyer should use me rather than existing internal resources! That means you should be able to quickly rattle off why you're a better alternative than someone like me!

✔ Things aren't happening as rapidly as I had hoped.

✔ We're experiencing more resistance from our people than I'd anticipated.

✔ Let's see how things work out at this stage before moving forward.

✔ My priorities have just changed.

Sound familiar? You need a response to every one, and others like them. But that's not difficult, because we've heard them all so many times. For example, take the fourth one. Here are some responses:

✔ Why do you think it failed previously?

✔ True, but four key conditions have changed.

✔ Actually, it worked, but was abandoned in the cost-cutting initiatives.

✔ It failed here, but worked for other departments (or the competition). Why do you think that occurred?

✔ And so on.

There are three reasons for everything. By that I mean that, psychologically, people tend to remember and be influenced by sets of three, or triads. So when you rebut an objection, have at least three clear and compelling rationales, and number them. That will usually win the day.

Finally, there is the classic "fish for" versus "teach to fish" dynamic, which I would like to elaborate on as shown in Figure 1.3.

From my perspective, the ideal dynamic is a diagonal line toward the upper right. That means that you are maximizing the importance of the issues on which you are working for clients *as well as* maximally transferring skills to the client to address such issues in the future. Again, this is an inherent advantage for the internal consultant. But too many internal people content themselves with far less valuable extremes, such as independent expert, analyst, or trainer.

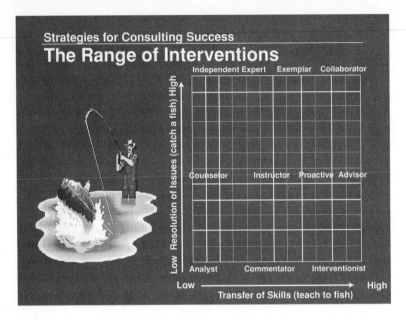

FIGURE 1.3 Expert position vs. skills transfer

The value for your clients—and for your future, combating the likes of me and my colleagues—is at the upper left.

These have been what I call the "basic dynamics" of consulting at the ground level. They aren't complicated and perhaps aren't elegant. But once you are *both comfortable and conversant* in the use of resistance to change, process versus content, the role of culture, and rebutting objections, you'll be a force to be reckoned with.

THE NATURE OF THE WORK

I want to conclude this initial discussion of the internal consulting role with some observations about the very nature of what we do as consultants.

The job involves three basic areas or dimensions. See Figure 1.4.

Physically, we probably need some measure of mobility, the ability to use a keyboard, powers of observation, and so on. There is no heavy lifting. And many physical shortcomings can be compensated

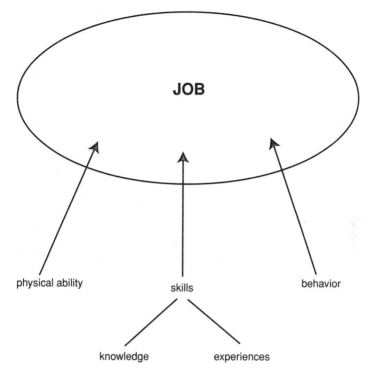

FIGURE 1.4 Elements of a job

for with technology, assistance, and so forth. From a skills (knowledge and experiences) standpoint, we need to master the elements of various consulting methodologies,[4] communications skills, and so forth. So we should be able to facilitate a meeting, moderate a focus group, interview people, create survey instruments, and so on.

Behaviors, however, often get short shrift. Few of us studied to be consultants, or had a lifelong passion to enter consulting. (I know I didn't, and look what happened to me.) The behaviors an internal consultant needs include, in my estimation:

[4]You may want to refer to my book *Process Consulting* from *The Ultimate Consultant Series*, Jossey-Bass/Pfeiffer, 2002. It contains a discussion of the various competencies of consulting expertise, how to acquire them, and how to implement them successfully.

✔ Perseverance: the willingness and resiliency to rebound from setbacks, to remove roadblocks, and to stay the course, even in the face of criticism and skepticism.

✔ High self-esteem: the ability to refuse to take rejection personally, and to disassociate one's own worth from scorn or negativism directed at one's department or colleagues.

✔ Well-developed sense of humor: Call this one perspective if you wish, but the truth is that nothing you or I do, no matter how successfully or unsuccessfully, is likely to change the course of civilization as we know it. We need to keep our wits about us.

> People succeed or fail at consulting not primarily because of skills, which are learnable, but rather due to behaviors, which are modifiable only within certain tolerances. If we don't have the correct behavioral set, we'll make others sick of us or sicken ourselves. That's what stress does.

✔ Willingness to take risks: no risk, no reward. "A highly conservative, successful consultant" is an oxymoron. Consultants aren't around to protect the status quo, although too many internal people seem to take that position. We're not here to stick our toes into the water. We're here to make waves.

✔ Creativity and innovation: This goes with the raising of the bar. The real value is in *improving standards and raising performance*. We need to be able to generate new ideas and better ways for our clients to adapt and implement.

Basically, the successful internal consultant will be at the confluence of these three factors: market need, competence, and passion (see Figure 1.5).

You need to be able to see (or create) the needs within the organization for the value you can provide; you must develop and demon-

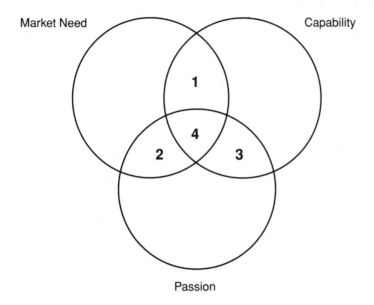

Market Need

Capability

Passion

FIGURE 1.5 Need, competence, and passion

strate the competency to meet those needs; and you must be passionate about the prospect of being the key link in that process.

It's as simple—and as achievable—as that. And as baseball pitching legend "Dizzy" Dean observed, "If you can do it, it ain't braggin'."

SUGGESTED READING

The Consultant's Calling by Geoffrey Bellman (Jossey-Bass, 1990) is a fine treatment of the philosophical basis and attitudinal requirements of the successful consultant. Not many books tackle that subject, and this one is a fine effort.

Creating Peer Relationships

How to Be Perceived as a Credible Partner by Line Management

ESCHEWING THE TOUCHIE-FEELIE NONSENSE

There has been no greater damage to the credibility, utility, and presumed sanity of internal consultants than the faddish approaches that have wasted money, spoiled reputations, and undermined respect over the 30 years I've been in this business. Other than that, I don't feel strongly about it.

In the first chapter we examined *why* it's important to be perceived as a peer of the line buyer. Now we'll talk about *how*. And the key aspect of that *how* is understanding *what not* to do.

Consulting is, by definition, a rather amorphous profession at worst, and multidisciplinary at best. That is, there are no simple templates and models that apply to most situations, and if you asked 12 quite adept consultants about the proper approach to, say, strategy formulation or population sampling, you'd likely get 18 respectable answers.

That's because there is no one royal road that forms the ideal consulting model leading from client need to resolution, or from today to tomorrow. There is, rather, a complex map that differing people can utilize for differing purposes: speed, safety, view, efficiency, and so on. But even on that varied map, there are dead ends, tortuous routes, and dangerous curves.

The bad roads on internal consulting have largely been the poorly designed, shabbily constructed, and soon-abandoned routes created by what I have termed the "touchie-feelie brigade." These are self-appointed gurus, one-trick ponies, former executives (whose success makes them think they have a magic formula to share), detached professors, aggressive consultants, and a host of others who have cutsie phrases and pseudo-research, *but who never have to actually do the job, and whose work is never held up to empirical or longitudinal scrutiny.*

> There is more arrant nonsense in the training and development profession than in almost any other outside of graphology and horoscopes. And I've seen training approaches that try to embrace graphology and horoscopes.

Many of you aren't going to enjoy hearing this, but the issue is so important to the success or failure of internal consulting that I'm going to run that risk with the hope of building your career. Here are just a few vivid examples of the bizarre and the pointless.

Right Brain/Left Brain Thinking. People are far too complex to be simplistically relegated to such superficial cognitive approaches. The most vocal advocate, the late Ned Hermann (creator of the Hermann "brain dominance" instruments) had to change his tune somewhat and cite his approach as a "metaphor" once the scientific community debunked much of the claims. This turned out to be another labeling exercise to help some people explain why they were better than others.

Future Search. Presumably a method to help planning and strategy formulation, this calls for participants to engage in an examination of seemingly unrelated events and times, going back in their history to consider their pet's name or their early habits. The trouble is that it's more than seemingly unrelated, it's totally unrelated. One of my clients, then a subsidiary of the Times Mirror Corporation, spent what I calculated as more than $400,000 of salaries trying to make this work, only to come up with complete garbage and a nearly mutinous group of otherwise rational managers. The highlight for me was when the two facilitators actually started arguing in front of the group about what to do next.

Diversity Training. First of all, diversity is not something anyone can be trained in. This is about beliefs and behaviors (as described previously with culture). Second, no one should be a diversity consultant. Diversity is an aspect of organizational effectiveness, no less than team work or problem solving. Anyone specializing in diversity without knowing basic organizational development is like someone trying to ski who only knows how to use the poles. Third, beware of any industry that grows up around a cause, and this is a primary example of one, with most practitioners having no special expertise or credentials other than leaping into the pond. Diversity issues and awareness should be an aspect of every organization's self-assessment, evaluations, performance goals, and so on, but not some isolated specialty. One great example occurred in the Federal Aviation Authority, where trainers asked participants to partially disrobe and smell each other's clothing, as well as require males to walk a gauntlet of females encouraged to shout abuse at them. The training was halted when employees, in a rational moment, filed suit.

Outdoor Experiences. These may be a lot of fun, but there isn't a scintilla of evidence that the results are transferable to the job, and most companies make an investment based on that premise, not on having fun. Tony Robbins, for one, has made a fortune, and is an engaging advocate, but walking on hot coals and rappelling down mountains does not translate to corporate needs.

Empty Motivational Rah-Rah. I love the speakers who tell you they used to be poor and now they're wealthy, and we're supposed to be improved by that fact. The reason they are now wealthy, of course, is that people are hiring them to go around telling that story, not because they've developed sophisticated, transferable skills for the audience. Most motivational workshops, courses, and speakers are of the sugar donut school of diet—a brief high, followed by zero lasting well-being or nutrition.

> Personality and behavior are too complex to be predictable under most circumstances, and certainly not from a $12 instrument that takes 10 minutes to complete. You might as well use one of those magic eightballs, which keep responding, "If you really believe in it," or "Is there any reason why not?"

Nonvalidated Tests and Behavioral Labels. If you want to call me a "high D" or a "driver-driver," or an INTJ on the cusp of Virgo, you had better do it with a running head start. Here's an eye-opener: To be valid, a behavioral or psychological test must have demonstrated construct, content, and concurrent validity, the proof of which must have been published in scientific, refereed journals. And even after that crucible, the test often must be revalidated for your particular organization and environment. Most of the popular tests on the market do not pass those criteria. As a result, we have internal trainers walking around giving feedback and diagnoses that a clinical psychologist wouldn't dare to offer. My favorite abuse: At Marine Midland Bank I found such an internal analyst asking executive questions that the former was trying to answer the way his deceased mother would have, so that the former could provide insights on the nature of their troubled relationship. I wanted to turn on the sprinkler system.

Pick your own favorites, but you get my point. You must avoid at all costs the fad-of-the-month, cute cliché, newest wonder book, and hot seminar. This business is about intellectual breadth, not jargonistic shallowness.

Case Study

The general manager of a $400 million division asked me to pursue a new craze called "open meetings," which was described (somewhat skeptically) in nothing less than the *Wall Street Journal*. I told him I had examined it and thought it was ridiculous. The idea was that people simply wandered around a room, voluntarily grouping themselves around easel sheets with topics they wanted to address. There was no other structure or design.

"Humor me," said the buyer, "and talk to the originator."

I tracked down the guy in Maine somewhere, and he told me by phone that his approach had a superb track record and everyone "loved it." I asked about times it didn't work, and he said there were none, which immediately raised every red flag in my flag locker. I asked for some client references, and he reluctantly gave me a few.

One reference told me that people had aimlessly drifted during the meeting and that most had settled around a topic about how to improve and increase compensation. The real corporate needs of increasing market share, improving technology, and retaining past customers never even made it onto an easel sheet.

"We ended the experiment right there," she said, "and the two people who advocated the approach lost so much credibility that I've advised them to think about leaving the company. The executives were furious and, by the way, we figure we lost $60,000 between the trainer's fee and the wasted morning."

I told my GM that story, suggested he forget about it, and he quickly did.

TAKING THE ROLE OF A PEER

If you successfully avoid the quicksand that sucks away credibility, then what are the positive steps to *gain* credibility? Remember that the primary drivers of dramatic internal consulting success are credibility, trust, and relationship building with line partners. Easier said than done, right?

Here's how you play the role of a peer. That is, here's how you become a colleague and not someone else's subordinate, despite job titles, office size, and amounts vested in the retirement plan. This is, after all, a relationship business, and you work in a public or private organization, not the military. Hierarchy is not enforced by epaulettes or courts martial.

> Executives want people around them who can help them meet their goals. The more valuable you are in that pursuit, the more you'll be invited to hang around. It's as simple as that.

Ten Steps to Peer Relationships

1. *Learn generic business terms and principles.*

Most human resources people seem to have trouble reading their own company's balance sheet, which is Accounting 101 and readily learnable. Understand what the P/E ratio means. Differentiate between earned and unearned income. Do you know what GAAP stands for, or cash vs. accrual? Are you familiar with cycle time, time-to-market, and just-in-time? Take a course or two if your company doesn't offer this very basic skills training. You need to talk the talk before you can walk the walk.

2. *Learn your organization's business terms and principles.*

Every organization has its own nomenclature and jargon. Amazingly, external consultants (at least the good ones) learn to master this quickly. Internal people should understand the terms that sales, IT, research, finance, manufacturing, and other areas use to communicate. There's nothing worse than to sit at a meeting and suddenly have a senior vice president turn to you and ask, "So how can you help us with our ASAC needs when customers are building straw men because of their own JIT demands?" Try to tap dance around that one. (Yes, I confronted that once. . . .)

3. *Never be defensive.*

Accept all feedback as constructively intentioned and potentially valid unless demonstrably proven otherwise. I've watched an executive state matter-of-factly, "We tried to improve delegation last year only to find that people were cynical of our intent," only to have one of the people responsible shoot back, "But that was because the senior people refused to go through the program first and we were refused the original budget request." People who see themselves as inferiors get very defensive; people who see themselves as peers seek constructive improvement: "You're right, and I'm concerned about that, too. I've developed three safeguards to prevent that from recurring, but I'd like your feedback and participation to make them most effective."

4. *When you speak, have something to say.*

People who feel insecure are often made highly uncomfortable when they're forced into silence, or haven't been able to contribute. As a result, they often blurt out nonsense or seek to fill silences with platitudes. By no means should you be unheard, but you must be heard saying something cogent and coherent. One of the worst scenarios is attempted humor that fails to amuse. Do some homework before a meeting, and have four or five key points you want to offer. You don't have to make them all, and one or two might be offered by someone else, since great minds think alike. But don't count on the extemporaneous or the sudden, blinding epiphany. Prepare in advance so that when you speak, people listen.

5. *Establish collaborations, not leg work.*

Whenever there's the opportunity for you to contribute, don't just run off and come back with your class project in a week, hoping for an A. Ask to sit down and compare some ideas. Request some conversation and brainstorming time. Play to ego: Tell them that it's not going to be very valuable if it's the result of you isolated in an office generating theoretical models. Start to educate your line partners that this is a collaboration, not an assignment.

6. *Judiciously push back.*

I have to laugh when I hear an internal consultant return from a meeting and say something like, "You won't believe what they've just decided to do!" Who was the consultant, an invisible fly on the wall? You must engage in what I call "push back," which is a gentle form of devil's advocacy. Here are the useful phrases:

- ✔ I'm sorry, but I need to challenge that basic assumption.
- ✔ What evidence do we have that this has ever worked at all?
- ✔ Why do you feel that way?
- ✔ Have you considered these risks even if we're successful?

These are all intelligent reactions to questionable logic and faulty premises. The people who raise them are inevitably appreciated by strong buyers.

> If you sit back and agree with nonsense, I can guarantee that you'll be the one blamed for either not stopping it or for having suggested it in the first place! It's far better to oppose lunacy at the outset, when it's clear that the idea isn't yours and you just might save the group money, time, and embarrassment.

7. *Don't go changing to try to please me (with apologies to Billy Joel).*

A sycophant is detectable three miles away by a stone. Sentient life is detectable even farther. Never cavil, bow, stoop, or otherwise genuflect to the management team. Don't go along for the ride if the idea is bad, but don't overly praise even good ideas. I actually saw a human resources guy tell the division general manager that he had better choices of shirts on casual Friday than any other man in the place. Two women in the room actually managed to role their eyes up above their eyebrows, like cartoon characters. And those two women were potential line buyers.

8. Accept the blame and share the credit.

This is what great leaders do. If something goes wrong, don't blame a lack of support from a key manager, or poor materials purchased from the outside, or the particular phase of the moon. Simply state that you hadn't anticipated correctly the degree of difficulty in implementing this uniformly across the field force, and here is the contingency plan you've developed to correct things. Conversely, when things are going well, readily share the credit (don't abdicate the credit, which is different) with the buyer's subordinates and peers. Demonstrate that this was a team and collegial approach.

9. Engage in lifelong learning.

While you should eschew the fads, don't overlook the need to continually improve. For example, it was recently documented that heterogeneous teams are more productive than homogeneous teams, which makes a strong case for the utility and pragmatism of diversity (and shows why the subject belongs in the general domain of organization development). There have been even more recent studies that begin to show a clear productivity improvement as a result of executive coaching, demonstrating that it's not a fad but rather a practical aspect of career development. If I know about this, shouldn't you?

10. Superb communications skills.

Finally and most grandly, learn to command a room. Never dumb down your vocabulary. Speak with expression. Listen with discernment. Use metaphors and analogies to support your points. Include judicious humor and always have a plethora of examples ready to bolster your arguments. We're all in the communications business these days, and we'd better get good at it. My observation is that people immedi-

---

If you can read with comprehension, write with expression, speak with influence, and listen with discernment you can control any discussion, any interaction, no matter who the other parties may be. At the very least, you'll hold your own as an admired peer.

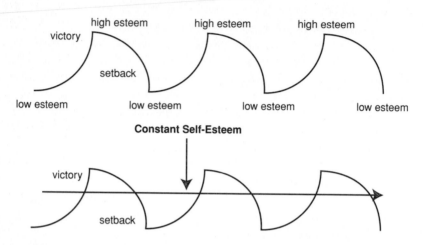

FIGURE 2.1   Self-esteem as a constant, not a roller coaster

ately respect others who can use the language well and colorfully. That's a learnable skill.

Most of all, you can't allow your self-esteem to become a roller coaster, as high as your last victory and as low as your last defeat. Your self-esteem must be constant, because you are confident about your skills and your role.

While it may seem simplistic to suggest within a half-chapter or so how you can be a peer of line management and economic buyers, think about whether you're doing what's suggested and avoiding what's cautioned. Very few internal staff people fit the profile just mentioned. The ones who do stand out in a crowd or in a meeting—and look good—every time.

PROACTIVE VERSUS REACTIVE ADVICE

One of the secrets of internal consulting is to be proactive. Most HR people, for example, content themselves to sit back and wait for line management requests, which they fulfill with pride. But this is a commodity mind set, and no more valuable than the pharmacist who fills the doctors' prescriptions.

It's far more helpful and valuable to be proactive, which means being diagnostic and not merely prescriptive. People often ask for the generic drug instead of the brand name to save money on the commodity, but they never say "Get me the cheapest internist" (or brain surgeon). The diagnostician is of great value, and we tend to follow the recommendations, no matter how painful.

The true calling of the internal consultant is not to *respond* but to *anticipate*. External consulting firms don't wait around to be called; they try to create need. Internal consulting operations are no different in that regard, yet have a potentially much more powerful asset—they know the organization intimately and should, therefore, be able to project need much more accurately.

No matter what request may come streaming in or what objective is imposed upon the consulting function, every internal consultant should be examining the following strategic considerations on a frequent basis:

✔ *How to make the best operations better.*

A common mistake is to focus on poorer operations. In fact, about 80 percent or more of all corporate developmental investment goes toward improving poor performers, rather than further exploiting strong performers. Consequently, the focus on internal consultants should be on raising the bar even higher for strong performers. If you'll forgive a baseball analogy, the benefits of improving a .310 hitter to .335 is far more beneficial than increasing a .210 hitter to .235. Don't fall into the trap of trying to analyze and improve poor operations. Instead, focus on the unusual: Make strong operations even stronger. The corporate contribution will be huge.

✔ *Break paradigms.*

Early in my career I was asked to chair a task force to determine which rental car company was best for our company's needs. In the midst of an arduous debate on frequency of use, the benefits of taking insurance coverage, and numbers of outlets, I suggested that we look at the alternative of requiring people to use taxis. After a nearly-acrimonious debate, a test was approved and, what do you know, the people using taxis exclusively had lower travel costs than people renting cars. Find better ways to do things, which may involve challenging existing beliefs and questioning present values.

✔ *Look outside the company at the environment.*

Organizations tend to be extremely introspective and self-centered. They fail to consider the competition, consumer trends, economic developments, technological improvements, and so on. Find those outside influences that may have the greatest effect on the success or failure of current strategy and offer suggestions on how to avoid, escape, tolerate, or exploit such external factors. In the United States, especially, consumer trends tend to accelerate or undermine even the best corporate strategies.

> A myriad of people will advise management to play it safe. Outside consultants are often attractive because they provide alternatives that involve greater return with prudent risk. Position yourself in that camp, and co-opt the interlopers. The great companies have not acquired that status by playing it safe.

✔ *Take risks.*

Staff functions are decidedly conservative. The legal people eschew anything that smacks of change, and the financial people want to eliminate risk altogether. This is not the formula of successful organizations (or careers). Seek dramatic ways to leverage sales, market share, time-to-market, and related high-impact areas. Become adept at risk/reward analyses. Figure 2.2 presents a quick example of one such model.

The key is to be able to demonstrate to management legitimate and attractive rewards while undergoing prudent and manageable risk.

Here is one method to ensure that your view is always fresh and unburdened by the conventional. Ask yourself these questions:

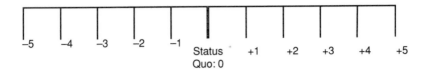

Question: What is the best and worst that might result?

+5 = Paradigm-breaking improvement, industry leader.
+4 = Dramatic improvement, major publicity.
+3 = Strong benefits, organization-wide.
+2 = Minor benefits, localized.
+1 = Very minor improvement, barely noticed.

−1 = Very minor setback, barely noticed.
−2 = Minor setback, controlled locally.
−3 = Public setback, requires damage control.
−4 = Major defeat, financial damages, recovery time needed.
−5 = Devastating losses.

FIGURE 2.2 A model for risk/reward assessments

- ✔ Why are we intent on doing this?
- ✔ What is the ultimate result to be achieved?
- ✔ What alternatives exist that can meet this goal?
- ✔ What alternatives can we create that can meet this goal?
- ✔ What risks are attendant to these alternatives?
- ✔ How may we mitigate or control those risks?
- ✔ What is the reward/risk comparison?
- ✔ How much risk are we willing to tolerate in return for how much benefit?

Note that "What are we doing now?" and "How can we expand what we're doing now?" don't enter this discussion. Paint a picture of the future and then determine how to get there. Don't simply extrapolate on the present, which produces much more restrictive results.

Case Study

I was working with a newspaper that had a chronic problem with "make goods," which are ads printed incorrectly, requiring the paper to either run them again correctly for free or return the fee. The paper was engaged in a lengthy and expensive debate about how to reduce make goods, including better training of ad placement people, a third level of proofing, and approved proofs sent to the advertiser.

All these alternatives were expensive, reducing the margins on the ad or forcing a price increase that would have made the ads noncompetitive.

Not knowing the business all that well, I suggested that the paper make the advertiser responsible for the ad accuracy by allowing them to directly place classified ads online. The advertiser submitted the ad, proofed it, and approved it, and any errors were the advertiser's fault, not the newspaper's, so make goods disappeared. Technology supported this alternative beautifully. In fact, the arrangement proved so successful that it was expanded to the more expensive display ads.

This is a technique known as "reversal." Try reversing accountabilities, deadlines, resource commitments, and so on. You never know how effective it may be until you try. You have to disassociate yourself from the status quo.

The best internal consultants act as if they have just landed on the planet, unaccustomed to the culture, the conventional, and the consistent. They examine alternatives, options, and the unprecedented. They are true nonconformists and iconoclasts.

AVOIDING THE IRS SYNDROME

"I'm from the IRS and I'm here to help you," has gone down in the lexicon of disingenuous statements. But "I'm from HR and here to help you" is not far behind.

My observations over the past quarter century is that HR hasn't really changed that much in terms of philosophy. Because of a lack of proactive stances and interventions, the function is viewed by employees as a shill of management, and by management as a biased advocate of employees. It's not easy to have both constituencies suspect your motives!

The management cynicism is largely a result of the "I'm sorry but you can't do that" school of thought. When a manager needs to hire people outside normal guidelines for exceptional circumstances, or needs to hurry through an appointment to meet a window of opportunity, or doesn't want to send people to mandatory training that bears no relevance for the operation, the best HR staffs find ways to accommodate the request, so long as it's legal, ethical, and not at the expense of other parties. But the worst departments play Big Brother, and decide that the means—the rules—are more important than the ends—the results.

> If a trade association isn't building the image and credibility of its members over the years, then what's the point of membership?

Moreover, HR is not well supported by one of the main professional trade associations, the American Society for Training and Development (ASTD), which has done little to foster standards or improve the quality of leadership other than stage conferences and events. For example, astonishingly, the ASTD doesn't even have the mechanism to throw out a member on the basis of ethical violations. The association believes in "aspirational ethics," whatever that means, and will not even remove people from membership for proven acts of plagiarism.[1]

---

[1]The Society for Human Resource Management (SHRM) is a far better outfit for certifying professionalism and improving standards.

Case Study

I was hired by a large manufacturer expressly to streamline the processes that enabled line management to identify, evaluate, extend offers, hire, develop, and retain new talent from the outside. I told the general manager that I was rather shocked that procedures weren't in place to do this, since there were very large staff functions in place.

"That's the problem," said the GM. "Every one of my directors—and there are eight with quite different personalities—tells me that they have to jump through hoops to find and acquire good people. Fix it."

What I found was that the human resources department had a farrago of forms, procedures, and processes in place, not to ensure rapid and quality acquisitions, but rather to guarantee that everyone experienced the same laborious and often meaningless steps. I recommended a collaboration, wherein line people established musts for the staff people to use in screening, and then were themselves responsible for the finer nuances once candidates passed the initial screen.

The HR people provided oversight to ensure that the laws and company guidelines were complied with (proper interviewing questions, proper reference checks, etc.) and that was that. The entire revamped recommendation took less than a week and was applied across-the-board.

The existing HR director went to the GM and said it wouldn't do, and that it was not going to happen on her watch. The GM said he understood, and fired her. Everyone else supported the new system totally after that.

The problem with the employee perception is that HR has not been in the forefront of leading change or even responding to abuse. In the case of racism at Texaco, sexual harassment at Astra, or massive layoffs at AT&T due to executive fiascos not employee productivity, HR wasn't anywhere to be seen or heard. And I've chosen these selections only because they were so egregiously public and broadcast.

Finally, the expertise of HR has been suspect, which has led to widescale use of ombudsmen, external Employee Assistance Programs (EAPs), external consultants, and outsourcing. In fact, transactional HR (benefits administration, moving and relocation, etc.) is a diminishing field. It's consultative HR that still holds some hope, and so we've come full circle to the real need.

Reaching the buyer constructively is a process, like any other. You must know where you are in that process and what's required to go to the next step. See Figure 2.3.

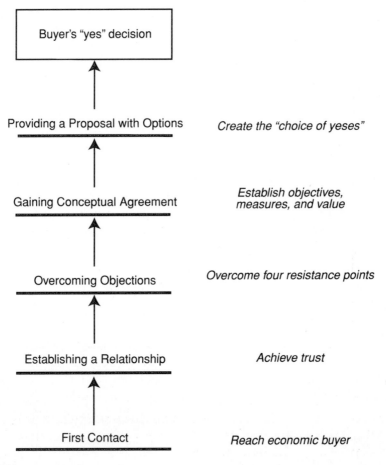

FIGURE 2.3 The process of reaching the buyer and gaining a "yes"

The relationship aspect is crucial, and the trust required demands that you methodically gain credibility, although that may not be in the traditional manner you expect.

The best ways to avoid the IRS syndrome and achieve credibility with the people who will hire you (management) and the people who will implement (employees) include:

- ✔ Take unpopular stands as required. You can't please everyone, and that's not the job anyway. Most external consultants who are really good will argue, debate, and push back at management. You can't be concerned about CRM[2] if you want to be respected.

- ✔ Don't show up only when there's a problem. (The IRS shows up to audit me, not to compliment me on my accurate reporting or to offer suggestions about how to minimize my taxes.) Inaugurate distinguished performance awards, provide feedback for excellence, and proactively provide ideas for improvement.

- ✔ Develop line relationships. Don't sit in the cafeteria with the same people you sit with during the rest of the day. Spend time developing ties with front-line people. Consider taking an extended rotation (e.g., 90 days) in a line area. Ideally, manage your career to include line management somewhere along the way.

> No one should confine their career to HR. The very best HR professionals I've ever met had spent significant time in other jobs. If you don't believe that, try teaching sales skills to a sales force that finds out you've never been in sales.

[2]Career Limiting Moves.

✔ Don't play "gotcha." Your job isn't to catch people, but to help people. You don't enforce rules for their own sake, but support rules intended to maximize performance toward corporate objectives (which include fairness, equity, ethical behavior, and so on).

✔ Develop the ability to take the pulse of the organization. Line management will find tremendous credibility in someone who can accurately reflect what the state of the organization is *and even more importantly predict what it's likely to be, given a certain scenario.* If you want that seat at the table, it's highly effective to point out, for example, that the new compensation system will pay more money for the same performance and will be ineffective in helping the people who are most inequitably treated.

✔ Span interest groups. Become familiar with the union, sales, R&D, manufacturing, call centers, remote offices, subsidiaries, and so on. Put yourself in the position to synthesize the organization's complexity and make sense of the interactions so that you can quickly discriminate between turf wars and legitimate conflicts of interest. Most leaders will see only their own landscape clearly. Become the person who can view the panorama.

✔ Read widely. You should be reading the *Wall Street Journal* and your local paper daily; *Fortune* or *Forbes* semi-monthly; industry newsletters and trade magazines monthly; and various Internet and collateral sources on a regular basis. I've been astounded when a manager will bring up a recent economic development and half the people in the room fall mute because they are either unaware of it or don't know how it relates to them or their organization.

✔ Become a leader in your profession. SHRM provides recognition at a certain level of performance (SPHR) and other honorifics. On the local level you can be a chapter officer. Publish in industry publications.[3] Serve as a speaker or

---

[3]Don't just publish in HR media, but in management media.

discussion leader at forums. Demonstrate that you're taking your position in the profession to higher and higher levels of excellence.

✔ Find a mentor. While many HR departments support mentoring programs, few of the professionals take advantage of them themselves. Identify a strong line manager who can serve to guide you and support you as an internal consultant and advisor.

✔ Become a strong coach. This is the converse of the previous point. "Executive coaching" has developed quite a bit of cachet, but is no fad. Executives have been coached by trusted advisors for as long as I've been in this profession. It's simply more recognized and publicly acceptable now (a sign of strength, not of weakness). There is no more valued internal consultant than the one who can serve as a discreet, intimate, and personal coach to powerful people.

> Internal people, imbued with the culture and history of the operation, are potentially the strongest imaginable coaches for executives. But the skills needed do not come from a certificate from some coaching school. They come from the combination of intellect, organizational knowledge, communications skills, confidence, and credibility that internal consultants should be constantly building.

We've now examined the role and relationships required to be an outstanding internal consultant. Let's turn now to the resources. Always bear in mind playwright Tom Stoppard's admonition: "Age is such a high price to pay for maturity."

SUGGESTED READING

The Capitalist Philosophers by Andrea Gabor (Times Business, 2000) is an excellent treatise on the movers and shakers in consulting, both internal and external, from Frederick Taylor and Mary Parker Follet to Elton Mayo and Peter Drucker. I use it in my graduate course for M.B.A. and Ph.D. candidates.

Tools of the Trade

What You Must Possess to Avoid Being Thrown out the Door

KEY BEHAVIORS

During the Civil War, Abraham Lincoln appointed George Mc-Clellan as the general commanding the main Union forces, the Army of the Potomac. This was the legion that was supposed to defeat Robert E. Lee after years of being battered by Lee under a succession of inept Union generals.

McClellan quickly impressed everyone with the levels of morale he created. He equipped the troops, drilled them, marched them past hundreds of congressional reviewing stands, and personally cut a dashing figure amidst the capital's social scene. He was nicknamed by the press the Little Napoleon.

Only Lincoln suspected trouble, because McClellan's dash was confined to a tight perimeter around Washington. When Lincoln badgered him to fight, McClellan always had an excuse—he was outnumbered, the training wasn't completed, his intelligence about the enemy was insufficient, the weather wasn't right. Ultimately, the general moved south with the agility of a behemoth, and was roundly defeated by Lee on several occasions. Lincoln replaced him with George Gordon Meade, who later won at Gettysburg and then served under Grant.[1]

McClellan had the skills to fight, but not the behaviors. He was meticulous, but not aggressive; he was patient, but had no sense of urgency; he oversaw detail well, but couldn't comprehend the larger picture.

We see people like this every day—otherwise wonderful fits for the job, but lacking the personality, volition, behaviors, and other ineffable traits required to actually get the job done. The salesperson who knows the product expertly, but can't bring himself to ask for the order; the entrepreneur whose research skills can create innovative products but who is uneasy working with others for funding and marketing; the natural athlete who chokes because she can't function well under pressure.

The same holds true for consultants. Most consultants who fail are not lacking skills or opportunity. They are lacking the behaviors that create success. You'll hear that external consultants mainly fail due to undercapitalization. Don't believe it. They fail because of poor self-esteem and the inability to deal with buyers as peers and partners.[2]

Internal consultants fail for similar reasons. They are usually quite adept technically, often certified in a gazillion programmatic interventions and constantly attending courses. But they don't appreciate or grasp the behavioral necessities for the job, and spend virtually no time developing *those essential elements*.

Superb consultants must be friendly without being cloying, and assertive without being belligerent. Sound like a fine wine? That's why outstanding internal consultants are so rare.

---

[1]McClellan went on to run for President against Lincoln in 1864 and was defeated as badly as if once again facing Robert E. Lee.

[2]My basis: More than 250 people through my mentoring program since 1996. This problem shocked me and caused me to reorient a great deal of my coaching away from technical skills and toward behavior modification.

What behaviors are required? Here are my candidates with some explanations attached.

High Degree of Assertiveness. In the sales lexicon, you have to be able to ask for the business. But equally important, you're dealing with people who may well outrank you with whom you want to establish peer level relationships. That doesn't come about from obsequiousness, sycophancy, or a "Yes, sir!" attitude. You should be able to hold your own, defend your beliefs, refuse to compromise on the ethical and quality criteria that protect your client.

You must have the spine to demonstrate that a project is ill-conceived or pursuing the wrong ends; that personality and turf conflicts must give way to finding cause and the organization's well-being; and that, while your client may be the expert in finance or manufacturing, you're the expert in consulting.

The secret to assertiveness: Never raise your voice, but back up what you say with factual evidence and observed behavior.

Case Study

I wanted a client so badly at one point, that I agreed to conduct a survey according to the client's criteria, even though I knew that the resultant instrument was a mishmash of poorly constructed questions and confusing instructions. But what I patched together from the client's demands pleased the buyer, so I blithely went ahead.

The survey results were a disaster, useful for very little, and the buyer blamed me. She brought in a larger firm to serve as her human resources strategy partner, and the firm confirmed (justifiably) that I had created a wreck of a survey.

What could I do, say that I was only following orders? My value as a consultant was negated by my determination to land a client at any cost. I got what I deserved—the door.

High Degree of Persuasiveness. Persuasion is needed more on the inside than the outside, because an external consultant is often already paid and has great leverage in threatening to walk away. But internal people can only walk to their offices, so persuasion is a better weapon than threat.

The key to consulting persuasiveness is *to demonstrate that the changes you seek are in the other person's self-interest.* No stakeholder is going to be too keen on change unless you can show that he or she will be demonstrably better off. That ability—to persuade and not demand—is the difference between commitment and compliance.

The secret of persuasiveness: Think from the outside in and determine ahead of time what self-interests you can best appeal to in order to create behavior change. (Hint: Ego is very powerful, but on the other person's part, not yours.)

The combination of low assertiveness and high persuasiveness makes one very approachable and an excellent counselor, such as a member of the clergy or a therapist. Your job is to seek ways for improvement, not to await patients at the door. Therefore, high assertiveness and persuasiveness are required.

Moderate to Low Patience Level. Consultants must be imbued with a sense of urgency. No matter what the reason for a project's delay—or, worse, failure—the consultant will be blamed. It's your job to move expeditiously and fine-tune in midflight, not on the ground.

I've learned a fascinating thing in my consulting career about urgency: You must move when you're about 80 percent ready. (See Figure 3.1.) This is because the final 20 percent of preparation is dysfunctional. The amount of time spent will never provide 100 percent perfection and, most critically, *the client doesn't know the difference.* That's right, the final 20 percent is not even recognized in the eye of the beholder, yet consultants fidget around forever trying to make certain

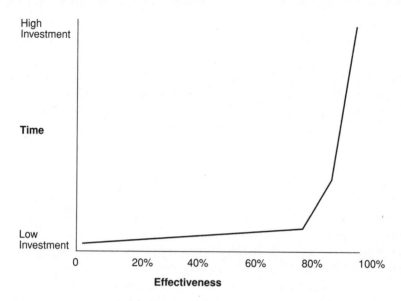

FIGURE 3.1 The wisdom of moving when 80 percent ready

that every loose end is tied in a perfect square knot. As we say in New York, fugeddaboudit.

The secret of urgency: Don't make elaborate project plans, but rather general mileposts that the client accepts but that you intend to beat every time.

As an external consultant, I've successfully balanced dozens of concurrent projects with diverse organizations situated all over the world. Please don't tell me that you can't juggle several projects within your own building. You must minimize detail and maximize results. That's the difference between being a consultant and a dilettante.

Moderate Attention to Detail. This might sound crazy, but it really doesn't matter if every *t* is crossed or *i* dotted. We're dealing with success, not perfection here. It doesn't matter if the new compensation system you designed to combat attrition doesn't have a colorful binder or separate website. It's minor if the focus groups aren't getting the refreshments promised while providing feedback on improving customer service. It's the decreased attrition and increased service that matter.

Delegate details, ideally to the implementers, or to administrative staff (although the latter is often a luxury these days). Don't allow yourself to be bogged down in the swamp of minutiae. Your buyer doesn't obsess over detail, and neither should you. Complete what's essential for the quality of the results, but don't sweat some of the mechanisms being less than perfect. Aircraft take off every day with small things wrong, so the likelihood is that your project will also fly even if something is squeaking or discolored.

One of the reasons that the vaunted quality movement exhausted itself was that the practitioners were too obsessed with issues *that never, ever reached the customer.* I can make a case that quality improvement is irrelevant if it doesn't impact the customer, and the same applies for almost any consulting intervention. Let's not confuse ends and means.

The secret of avoiding detail paralysis: Ask yourself, "Does this affect the quality of the results in the eyes of the customer, or is the imperfection hidden and unknown to the end user?"

If you can master high assertiveness and persuasiveness, moderate patience, and comfort with relatively low detail, you're situated in a great place behaviorally. If you can't, then *that's* the kind of coaching, mentoring, and development you need, not your umpteenth coaching certificate from Coaches R Us.

There are other behaviors that help, and I'll mention them briefly:

- ✔ Flexibility: the comfort in finding more than one avenue to reach the same destination.
- ✔ Resilience: the ability to bounce back from defeat and/or rejection.
- ✔ Perspective: the ease to place life and work in balance so that pressure doesn't overwhelm you.
- ✔ Humor: the ability to defuse a situation by helping everyone lighten up and reduce stress.

MANDATORY SKILLS

I'm constantly asked what model I employ in my consulting, and I'm then challenged to explain that consulting is a process that may or may not incorporate varying models but is not a model in and of itself. We look at the key processes in a later chapter.

There are skills, of course, that are critically needed by anyone calling herself a consultant, but some of those skills my surprise you. There are surprisingly few that I'd cite as mandatory, and they're not about running focus groups or rearranging the room so that people feel empowered.

Framing Skills. The single most important skill I've utilized is that of "framing." Framing means helping the client (and yourself) see the picture by throwing cogent and logical boundaries around it. I can frame a client's issue in the first two minutes of any substantive discussion. Some consultants launch projects without ever having done so.

> Throw a different light or angle on the issues and the client will look at the landscape from a new perspective. Your ability to eliminate shadows and uncertainties and to shine bright light in troublesome corners creates instant value and authority.

Clients (especially internally, where they expect you to understand the culture, lingo, and history immediately—I'm under no such pressure, since I'm an uneducated outsider, a huge advantage) will "core dump" everything they know about their problem, issue, or opportunity. After a few minutes of listening (most of which isn't to hear more but just to be polite by not cutting in too soon), outstanding consultants say, "In other words, your new sales levels are being undercut by unprecedented customer desertion." Or: "If I've heard you correctly, time-to-market is being delayed because there is no incentive tied to the commercialization of R&D work."

You must be able to quickly paraphrase and succinctly create the real challenge. That ability will instantly prompt the client to believe you have great insight and analytic ability, and will dramatically elevate your credibility. You know a client is impressed when he or she says any of the following:

"You've expressed it better than I could."

"You've grasped the issue more quickly than most people."

"That's brilliant—I've never looked at it that way before."

Diagnostic Participative Skills. There is nothing as powerful as co-opting the buyer to join you in the diagnosis so that you are jointly party to the buying decision. This creates instant peer relationships. The good news is that this is a learnable skill. The bad news is that most people have never mastered the tools.

The essential element here is to provide a basis within which you and the buyer can quickly—and the operative word is "quickly"—

Case Study

A prospective buyer asked me to describe a communications strategy for his post-merger world (as I've correctly assumed he'd asked another dozen consultants).

"Why would you want that?" I said, "since you have virtually nothing to say. You've told me you don't know which offices will close, which officers will be in charge, or even which benefit system will survive."

"So, what are you suggesting?"

"You need a *listening* strategy. You have nothing to say, but you must find out what employees are thinking and let them know you've heard them so that they can get back to work and post-merger productivity rebounds."

"Why, that's counterintuitive!" he stammered.

I got the job. I had shone a different light on what the buyer had thought was a static (and unappealing) landscape.

> Don't be prescriptive. Then you're merely a pharmacist fulfill-
> ing some doctor's scrawled orders. Be an internist, and work
> with your client to jointly diagnose the issues. Prescriptive
> help is a *commodity*. Diagnostic help is of huge *value*.

assess the current situation. I use tools I've termed "process visuals" to do this.[3]

Here's just one example. (See Figure 3.2.)

If a buyer is talking to me about productivity, for example, I'll draw Figure 3.2 and ask how much of the unit's time is spent on exter-nal activities (product, service, relationship, customer, etc.) and how much is spent on internal activities (concerns about the compensation plan, unhappiness with a turf rival, administrative nonsense, etc.). I point out that the ratio ought to be 10 percent internal and 90 percent external. The buyer develops his or her own assessment (usually pretty bad) and we agree that even a modest shift to a more external focus will be a productivity bonanza with no capital investment.

Such devices are even easier for you, as an internal consultant, since you probably have facts and data to support certain positions. In any case, once the buyer is hooked on being in a poorer situation than is achievable within the model, the decision shifts to how to improve, not whether to do it.

You need to master as many of these simple tools as appropriate for the types of concerns you face (I have hundreds that I can sponta-neously draw on a moment's notice, as if I had just thought of them). You're successful when the buyer says:

"We need to move to your upper left quadrant in the model."

"This is a great performance metric, and we need something like it."

"I wish I had seen things in this light before."

---

[3]See my book *The Great Big Book of Process Visuals, or Give Me A Double Axis Chart and I Can Rule the World* (Summit Consulting Group, Inc., 2000). I describe 50 such tools, with their origins and uses, and include a CD so that you can transfer them to your own work.

100% of the organization's
talent and energies
focused externally

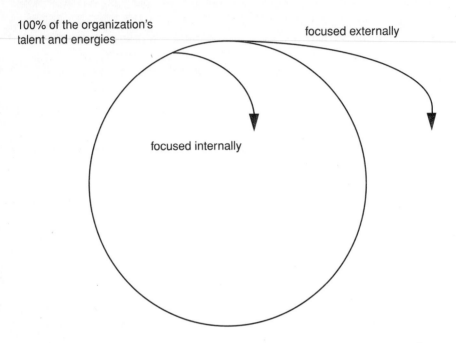

focused internally

FIGURE 3.2 A process visual—an opportunity for joint diagnosis with the buyer

Conflict Resolution. There is inevitable conflict during consulting projects—conflict among stakeholders, among sponsors and the buyer, and between you and the buyer. Not everyone's interest is the same or even compatible.

Conflict is unavoidable, so you might as well become adept at resolving it, which is why this is the final component in our unlikely skills pantheon.

The key here is counterintuitive: Few true conflicts are about personality. Poor chemistry and battling egos do play a small role, but the preponderance of conflict occurs over two issues:

1. Disagreement about objectives.
2. Disagreement about alternatives.

If you can sort out the source of the conflict quickly (see the framing skills mentioned previously), you can resolve it rapidly, because each type of conflict has its own unique starting point.

> Consultants generally don't lack *implementation* skills. They lack *project safeguard* skills, to coin a term. There is more success with a mediocre methodology and all parties strongly in support than there is with a brilliant methodology and all parties at war. Consulting is not about perfection of delivery, but about success in garnering support.

Conflict about Objectives. This occurs when two or more parties disagree about the end goals and is by far the more serious conflict of the two. The buyer might seek to expand the number of customers in the Northeast while one or more subordinates believe that the goal should be fewer sales at higher prices. These are profoundly differing destinations, requiring radically different approaches in pricing, training, marketing, and so on.

To resolve this type of conflict, you must establish who the owner of the process is (it may, in fact, not be the buyer if the vice president for Northeast operations is the sole executive affected). That owner should have the final say about the desired end results, unless the project is to correct some egregious problem the owner has already caused.

Unresolved conflict about objectives will kill any project, because key players will refuse to cooperate on what they see as quite reasonable and ethical grounds: The ends don't justify the means. Your job here is to deliver a consensus around the legitimate ends.

Conflict about Alternatives. In this case, the ends are agreed upon but the route to achieve them is disputed. The goal of expanding the customer base in the Northeast may be met by bringing on noncustomers, stealing market share from competitors, or creating entirely new products to appeal to new demographics altogether.

Here the goal is to find the alternative(s) that best meet the objectives within acceptable risk limits. (Every alternative has residual risk since nothing is a sure thing or there'd be no need to plan at all.) To resolve this type of conflict, ask the interested parties to engage in a risk/reward analysis, which you facilitate. Evaluate each option's merits versus its threat, and arrive at a prudent decision.

Unresolved conflict about alternatives will generate halfhearted responses and even competing entries in the race. Your job here is to prove that a given alternative is superior to others in meeting the agreed-upon objectives.

You're successful in resolving conflict when participants say:

"I'm comfortable that we've examined all options and suggestions objectively."

"We're all on the same page now, agree on goals."

"I can support this and explain it to my people logically."

Framing skills, diagnostic participation skills, and conflict resolution—perhaps not the set of skills you had anticipated at this point. But that's why internal consulting is so often unsuccessful. People are developing arcane skills in implementation when it's actually the skills of defining issues and building consensus around approaches to them that carry the day.

USEFUL EXPERIENCE

There are some delivery and implementation experiences that stand us all in good stead. What should a good internal consultant be experienced in delivering or executing?[4]

✔ Focus groups: You should know the essentials of selecting participants, establishing the proper environment, facilitating, analyzing, and reporting on focus group sampling.

---

[4]For far more detail on specific disciplines, see my book, *Process Consulting* (Jossey-Bass, 2002).

✔ Interviewing: The ability to conversationally and nonthreateningly interview anyone from a production line worker to the CEO.

✔ Surveys: The competence to understand what information is required for what end purpose, developing the correct instrument, administering, collating, evaluating, and reporting results.

The more ammunition in your arsenal, the more targets you can shoot at. Specific consulting skills are generally easy to learn and practice. If you're a one-trick pony or attempting to wing it, better get out of the way, because someone will be hired to do it the right way.

✔ Facilitation: The ability to run a meeting without taking sides, to acknowledge and embrace differing points of view, to proceed sequentially through an agenda stimulating conversation while suppressing duplication and irrelevance, and to provide all participating with the beliefs that they were heard and were involved in honest debate. Good facilitators find cause not blame, and focus on future actions not past reprisals.

✔ Planning and project management: Both of these pursuits involve the organization and priority setting that propel and plan forward, anticipating and resolving roadblocks and resistance. Preventive actions should be in place to avoid trouble, but contingent actions should also be established to handle the unavoidable.

✔ Team building: The ability to set rules of engagement for teams, to support and develop team leaders, to identify and correct inhibiting behaviors, and to ultimately create self-sanctioning, self-directed teams that establish their own goals, priorities, and work flow.

✔ Coaching: The best coach can work with any level of individual, and establishes objectives for improvement, metrics to measure success, and an enduring discipline to reinforce new, positive habits and behaviors. Coaching should be confidential, tailored, and flexible. It's more important to have trust and a firm grip on improvement objectives than is a certificate from a coaching school and an inflexible methodology to go with it.

✔ Training and development: The creation of learning objectives and course curricula and exercises to meet those objectives, including criteria to measure success. This may include self-paced instruction, remote learning, and other forms of development in addition to traditional classroom training.

✔ Succession planning and career development: The ability to synthesize the top-down needs of the organization (succession planning) with the bottom-up needs of individuals (career planning). These two disciplines shouldn't cross unaware, like ships in the night. A key is the identification of future needs, and not a reliance on yesterday's demands.

> You're better off being conversant in a tried-and-true need than expert in a fad. Just how many future search, right brain/left brain thinkers, or transactional analysis experts are in demand today?

There are other skills you may add to my list, but if you master my core assembly, you're in fine shape. Note that specialties such as wages and benefits, relocation, recruiting, and so on are increasingly outsourced and of less value. You need to master the consultative side, not the transactional side.

INTELLECTUAL ARMAMENT

What we do is about intellectual breadth. Company knowledge and business acumen are important, but the ability to relate to the world around us is even more critical. After all, there is very little new under the sun. The Egyptians building the pyramids were concerned about just-in-time delivery, and the Roman legions relied on teamwork extensively.

But what is new—and vitally important—is our ability to relate ideas about strategy, tactics, development, education, and other consulting methodologies to:

- ✔ The contemporary society, with its mores, values, and beliefs.
- ✔ The contemporary technology, with its advantages of communication and disadvantages of impersonality and diversion.
- ✔ The contemporary economy, with its volatile movements and interconnectedness.
- ✔ The diversity that increases among both customers and employees.
- ✔ The globalization of business, which is affecting even mom-and-pop operations, let alone major organizations.

While the process of, say, decision making, is unchanged despite time (it revolves around objectives, alternatives, and risk, no matter what model you favor), as a process it must be applied differently (1) when people aren't looking at each other but communicating across time zones electronically; (2) when people are contributing who have varying cultural reference points; (3) when the economy dictates that high risk may not be acceptable or that low risk is too conservative; or (4) when different cultures will react in differing ways to the same message.

The challenge, then, is to best apply the tools of the trade to the vicissitudes of the time. And there is even a more volatile problem today.

There are basically two strata of managers in today's corporations. There are those who are in their fifties to sixties, and who progressed to their current positions without having to master technology, global trade, diverse demographics, or instantaneous communications. They are now somewhat at sea, and while the very best of them surround themselves with outstanding help, most of them muddle through or fake it.

Case Study

While engaged in a project for Marine Midland Bank in the 1990s on the integration of technology employed by the bank, I found myself interviewing each member of the office of the chairman to determine how these powerful people used technology.

None did, with the exception of my last interview, an executive vice president with a computer on his credenza, unprecedented at his level.

"You find it helpful?" I asked.

"Oh, I'm a believer in advanced technology," he assured me.

I asked for a demonstration of how he used it and, strangely, he pressed a button on his desk. I had never seen such a setup, until I realized that the button summoned his secretary, who had quickly entered the office.

"Edith," he said, "show Mr. Weiss how we use the computer while I run along to my four o'clock conference, would you?"

We're faced with managers who are unaccustomed to contemporary changes but have managed through bad times, and managers who are accustomed to contemporary changes but have only managed through good times. Are you still willing to tell me that you have trouble finding clients?

Then there are those managers who are in their thirties to forties who have grown up with technology, diversity, global trade, and all the other contemporary shifts. But virtually none of this cohort has managed in bad times. They were appointed and grew during the boom 1990s, and the turbulence and uncertainty of a volatile economy are unknown to them.

My point is that there is plenty of potential business out there— actually more than enough for both internal and external consultants who bring separate strengths to the equation—so finding clients shouldn't be the issue. That is, unless you've fallen behind in keeping up with your potential partners.

As I write this, there are about 280 million people in the United States, who currently support a $10 trillion economy. Social Security is in trouble because the demographics supporting it are from the 1940s, when about 11 people worked for every retiree, and people retired at 65 with a life expectancy of 68. Today there are only about three people working for every retiree, and people retire much earlier on average and live well into their seventies.

How much of this do you know? How well-versed are you in the context of our times?

Here is my highly subjective but I think powerful recommendation for your intellectual development:

✔ Read the *Wall Street Journal* every day. I've found that I can get it anywhere in the world, even if it's a day late and costs five dollars. This is probably the finest written newspaper in the country, and includes important information about the arts, politics, technology, investing, and so on besides pure business news. It's negligent—unforgivable—for a consultant not to make this daily reading.

✔ Read every issue of *Business Week* or *Industry Week*. I prefer the former. You'll receive a pithy digest of what's happening to affect the business community.

✔ Read *Fortune* or *Forbes* regularly. You'll find more in-depth news about business and industry.

✔ Read publications in the fields of consulting, training, and development to stay apprised of the state-of-the-art. This might include *Training, Training & Development Journal, C2M (Consulting to Management*—I know, it's a dumb name), *Human Resource Executive, HRMagazine*, psychology abstracts and articles, and so forth. You have to be able to separate the trite from the significant. (For example, validated tests must appear in a refereed journal, with validation studies.)

✔ Read a minimum of 4 of the 10 books on both the *New York Times* fiction and nonfiction lists. This will provide tremendous insights into what people are interested in as well as the ammunition to conduct conversations about what's popular and/or important (not necessarily the same thing).

✔ Read your local newspaper every day. Find out what's happening around you. Don't rely on televised sound bites.

> Being well-read and well-informed makes you an object of interest to others, which develops better relationships, which fosters greater trust, which leads to true partnerships. And besides, you might just enjoy yourself.

Reading widely and developing your intellect are excellent advantages to making you a better consultant, more valuable resource, and superb candidate for advancement.

These are the tools of the trade, and this has been the environment in which we operate. Now let's turn to the interactions that make or break consulting engagements.

SUGGESTED READING

The Mager Library by Bob Mager (Pittman Learning, 1984). Bob Mager is simply one of the most brilliant (and funniest) writers about learning and design ever to put pen to paper. His classic about learning objectives, *You Really Oughta Wanna*, is included in this compendium, which features a photo of his face on the front cover, and a photo of the back of his head on the rear cover.

PART TWO

THE INTERACTIONS

The Role of Conceptual Agreement

The Absolutely Best Way to Establish a Win/Win Project

RELATIONSHIP BUILDING

The most important factor in landing consulting assignments, whether as an internal or external resource, is not the price, the methodology, or the close, contrary to popular mythology.

It's the relationship.

Ironically, the more time invested in building relationships with potential buyers, the more you actually accelerate business in the long term. That's because strong relationships prevent superficial arguments over technique, avoid doubts and mistrust, and mitigate concerns over costs and timing. Relationships are the keys that open the doors to value.

The sequence—and keystone role of relationships—is illustrated in Figure 4.1. Here are the definitions:

Values. Those business beliefs that are shared by buyer and consultant. These are not spiritual, but pragmatic. If a buyer wants to

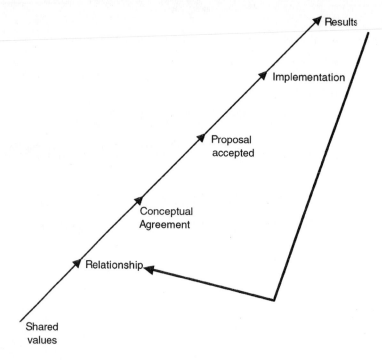

FIGURE 4.1   The sales sequence

conceal impending layoffs and build morale through subterfuge, you have the obligation to refuse to collaborate (assuming you don't share the belief system that allows for such practices). It's not suicide to turn down a request that is anathema to your value system. In fact, it's usually fatal to comply with requests you know are wrong and can't support.

Relationship. A peer-to-peer level of understanding and respect that enables both parties to communicate openly and honestly. This means that either can disagree with the other without jeopardizing standing or past agreements. Relationships are not based on hierarchical parity but rather on the belief that each person has something of genuine value to offer the other. Above all, they rely on trust and honesty (see the following section).

> When the buyer stipulates the value, the consultant has no
> need to provide justification for charge backs, disruptions, or
> attendant costs. But only the buyer can express true value *as
> it pertains to him or to her.*

Conceptual Agreement. This is a stated agreement on project objectives (business outcomes), measures of success (metrics), and value to the buyer (ROI). This, too, will be discussed in detail later in this chapter.

Proposal. Every consulting project should be summarized in a proposal, but no proposal is appropriate prior to conceptual agreement. Proposals are summations, not explorations. The proposal protects both parties as well as providing a template to avoid "scope creep" and other hazards.[1]

Implementation. The project is implemented in accordance with proposal specifics.

Results. The business objectives are met as determined by the metrics and the agreed-upon value is delivered. This reinforces the relationship, since the consultant did what was promised with the intended results. This is why relationships are self-perpetuating, and are an internal consultant's most important marketing device.

Bear in mind that such progression is almost always a sequence of small yeses, and rarely a giant gulp from initial meeting to contract (unless you have a prior history with the buyer).

Relationships are of tremendous advantage to internal consultants. External consultants have no prior relationships (at least in new prospects) and must work to formulate positive relationships in a relatively brief span and always with the looming potential project

---

[1]For detailed discussion on all aspects of proposal writing, including sample templates on CD, see my book *How to Write A Proposal That's Accepted Every Time, Best Practices Series* (Kennedy Information, 1999).

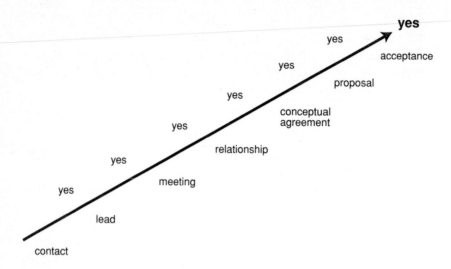

FIGURE 4.2   The series of small yeses

in view. It's a real balancing act. (Take it from a veteran high-wire performer.)

But internal consultants have the huge advantage of building relationships daily, not dependent on the emergence of a project or request. *Yet most internal consultants completely ignore this huge marketing leverage, and have no better internal relationships (or worse ones) than an external consultant entering the environment.*

If I ran an internal consulting operation, my marching orders to the staff would be as follows:

- ✔ Every week develop new relationships with prospective line clients. Offer them value, interact with them about business issues, have lunch with them, be visible—on their radar screens.

- ✔ Every week reinforce the relationships you already have with line clients. Follow up on past work, offer new suggestions, serve as a coach, see them regularly, and don't disappear from their radar screens.

It's astounding to me how internal change agents act like groundhogs, seldom venturing from their burrows unless disturbed and, even then, retreating for weeks if they see a shadow—anyone's shadow.

Internal consultants should have excellent relationships with every prospective line client they can identify. Too often, they spend time with each other, or with relatively low-level people (hierarchical peers), who are glad to see them but can't buy from them.

If these relationships are strong and continually nurtured, you accelerate through the sales sequence directly to conceptual agreement, a huge advantage. (And in developing those relationships, you may discover some potential clients whose value systems preclude your desire to work with them. That, too, is useful.)

Suggestion: Perform an inventory of your friendships, acquaintances, and relationships in your organization. If the potential line customers are noticeably in the minority, or even absent, then you have a lot more relationship building to do. Don't just hang out with people who look like you, speak like you, and work with you. Those aren't your customers.

TRUST

Relationships are founded on trust. They are never founded on obsequiousness, sycophancy, or fawning.

Trust is the absolute, unswerving belief that the other person has your own best interests in mind. This means that disagreements, debate, support, questioning, anger, surprise, and virtually any other emotion or reaction are accepted in the context of constructive support.

If I oppose you, and you trust me, you'll listen carefully to my arguments. If I oppose you, and you don't trust me, you'll find ways to overcome me. (And if you hold superior rank in the organization, it's easy to overcome me.)

In order to gain conceptual agreement, there must be trust. Potential clients and partners are not going to share with you their true objectives, fears, beliefs, and insights if they don't trust that you are an honest and objective partner.

How does an internal change agent or consultant gain trust with people who are normally outside their influence and perhaps even daily dealings?

Ten Steps to Trust

1. Show up. Trust takes time, so build it in advance. I was at a meeting where a general manager asked an internal consultant what company he worked for. When the latter replied, "This one," the general manager said, "You must be fairly new. I know everyone at this site." Everyone else lost eye contact, knowing that the consultant had worked there for three years. Meet people on a regular basis. Speak out at meetings. Get on the radar screen.

2. Make intelligent noises. It's not good to stand out in a crowd if the reason for the spotlight is that the crowd is shunning you. Do some homework and make insightful suggestions at meetings. Don't fill silences with dumb comments because the situation makes you feel awkward. Build your personal and business vocabulary so that you communicate superbly. A vice president stopped a meeting once to ask what a word I had just used ("tendentious") meant. The rest of the participants were stunned, but I was content to stand out in a room that had otherwise dumbed itself down.

It's true that trust is earned, not demanded, but it's also true that the process can be accelerated by doing the things that enhance trust and avoiding the things that undermine it. On balance, are you building it or eroding it each day?

3. Blow your own horn. If you don't blow your own horn, there won't be any music. Publish in the house newsletter, magazine, or other internal media. Serve as a facilitator or master of ceremonies at company events. Volunteer to lead a fund drive or service in the community on behalf of the company. Don't proclaim how good you are, but do demonstrate how involved and informed you are.

4. Create your own pedigree. Your department or function might have a credibility problem. Don't allow that to subsume you. If HR has a bad reputation, don't merely tell people you're from the HR department. Tell them you're an internal consulting specialist, or a divisional change agent, or a change facilitator, or whatever you choose to create for yourself. Create separate business cards if you can. Don't carry someone else's baggage if you don't have to.

5. Can the honorifics. I received a letter from someone last week whose name had no less than *six* sets of initials after it, something like: C.P.C.M., C.M.W., R.V.P.(sm), M.A., L.P.G., S.C.M. Do you know what impressed me—how much of a fraud he probably is. Your potential clients recognize Ph.D., M.A., M.B.A., and a couple of other things. Don't try to dazzle them with footwork, because generally, the more initials, the less substance.

6. Eschew the fads. Once you start talking about right-brain/left-brain thinking, open meetings, future search, high D personalities, or any other faddish and totally useless stuff, you're going to be assigned to the "don't call us, we'll call you" list. Don't fall into the black hole of the cult mentalities.

7. Learn the issues. One of my clients has a catch line that asks, "What do you really care about?" What key and critical issues are your potential partners facing? Do they concern market share, commercialization of R&D, talent retention, global competition? There's a huge difference between walking into a meeting and discussing collapsing sales closing time, and discussing how rearranging the conference room will redistribute power.

8. Catch a wave. What are the hot company initiatives, which may well incur risk, the early supporters of which will gain tremendous credibility if all goes well? Is there site expansion, new technology, new products or services, or a reorganization that might make you a hero? What may vault you to prominence and prompt others to trust in your judgment and competence?

9. Act dispassionately. The Enron/Andersen debacle underscored the importance of independent, objective, and trustworthy advisors. This doesn't necessarily imply that those advisors must be external, especially for consulting help. In fact, good internal people should have the trust advantage over good external people (though sadly this is often not the case). Don't take sides or allow yourself to be thrust onto a position purely for political reasons. Go with the flow when you believe in the cause, but stand aside and protest when you don't. Remember Thomas Jefferson's admonition: "In matters of taste, swim with the tide; in matters of principle, stand like a rock."

10. Provide proactive value. Without invitation and without an external prompt, find some value to deliver to your potential line partners. The value must be something appropriate for their positions and levels of concern. A book or technique on team building will be shuttled to a subordinate. But a tweak in the sales compensation system that could generate more sales earlier in the year—alleviating the traditional fourth quarter scramble—will get the rapt attention of any executive. The opportunities actually abound. What's missing is the volition to exploit them.

> Trust is in the eye of the beholder. "What's in it for her?" is the question that must precede any notion of what's in it for you.

Some final thoughts on trust: Henry Thoreau once said that He serves the state best who opposes it the most. I'm not sure that you have to oppose the state (corporation), but you do have to oppose the illegal, immoral, unethical, unprofitable, and just plain dumb.

I spend more time than I ever imagined telling new clients, "Stop doing that. Why on earth are you doing that?" (I generally lose eye contact with everyone else in the room.) When an external resource has to tell management that it's done something stupid, there is a very pungent, unmistakable odor resulting, which indicates those who knew about this and said nothing are really the ones who are culpable.

And that target is quite often the human resources department.

I've seen HR dutifully assist in implementing call center reorganizations that they knew would infuriate clients; compensation systems that they knew would not improve sales but would increase commissions, thereby lowering margins; training programs that had no design objectives, no metrics for measuring impact, and no ultimate connection with any changed behavior or improved performance. These boondoggles have taken their toll.

It's insufficient to say, "I tried to tell you, but you wouldn't listen," or "I'm not going to go up against a vice president," or "That would be a career-limiting move." The true career-limiting move lies in doing nothing and in acceding to bad plans, selfish requests, and stupid gambles. It's safe to say that when a rocket explodes, directors are not going to ask the people who built and maintained it to build the next one on the basis that they've now learned so much. They're going to bring in someone who says, "You don't use a rocket for this; you use a telephone."

The only harder thing than building trust is *rebuilding* trust that's been lost. The unfortunate truth—and I'm trying to provide you with the dispassionate truth here as someone considering your best interests—is that a great deal of trust has already been sacrificed. That's why you have to be proactive and aggressive in re-establishing it.

OBJECTIVES, MEASURES, AND VALUE

The core to my consulting methodology is to establish objectives, measures, and value with the buyer. I call this "conceptual agreement." If you have agreement in concept, then the ensuing project has strong assurances of success. Excellent external consultants always generate

> Conceptual agreement makes the ultimate proposal a simple summation, not an exploration. The time to reach agreement with your buyer is in conversational, peer-level discussion, not in some formalized document or contract.

conceptual agreement (even though they might call it something else), but internal consultants seldom pursue it.

The elements are quite simple:

Objectives. These are always business outcomes that the buyer seeks to achieve. They are *never* deliverables, methodologies, or technologies. For example, improving client retention is a business objective, but sales manuals, focus groups, surveys, and "a better understanding of client needs" are simply steps along the way and inherently of less value.

Measures. These are the metrics against which success can be measured. They serve as progress points and also a connection with you as the catalyst of success. The human resources community has long been under the mistaken notion that there are "four levels" of measurement, as originally espoused by an academic, a professor named Donald Kirkpatrick. Those measures, supposedly, are of learning, attitude, behavior, and results.

In fact, the *only* measure of any relevance at all is results. If people's attitudes (or behaviors or learning) change, but there is no demonstrable change in business outcomes, then the intervention is senseless and, well, academic. And the exact problem with most training programs extant—perhaps as much as 90 percent of them—is that they do not produce any clear improvement in business results (much less results against predetermined objectives). "Smile sheets" and course evaluations are not only meaningless; they are stupid. The only person to ask is the manager of the student, not the student. (If you measure whether people like a course, then instructors will orient their behavior around that evaluation, and will seek pleasant experiences rather than changes in results, which are often painful and unpopular.)

Value. The powerful nuance within conceptual agreement is *to prompt the buyer to stipulate the value to him or her, and/or to the organization.* Once the buyer stipulates the value, the cost of the intervention is irrelevant. An input, such as a training manual, will always have limited value, but the result of increased sales will have dramatic value. Buyers will gladly tolerate otherwise objectionable factors—their own time investment, organization disruption, complaints from subordinates, just to name a few—if the overarching value is clear and profound. For external consultants, this justifies high fees. For internal consultants, this justifies high levels of commitment, disruptions, support, and so on.

Essentially, the buyer must see clear value with a fixed investment, and not vague benefits with clear costs. (Hence the need to eschew the touchie-feelie nonsense of personality profiles and rearranging the meeting tables.) Figure 4.3 shows what that relationship looks like.

Conceptual agreement achieves the following:

✔ Gains the support of the buyer.
✔ Enables the buyer to sell the intervention to subordinates.

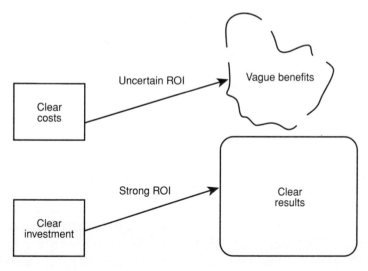

FIGURE 4.3   Establishing clear ROI rather than prohibitive costs

✔ Justifies discomfort (disruption, investment, unpopularity, etc.).

✔ Prevents scope creep, since the goals are clear.

✔ Effectively closes the sale.

✔ Provides a guideline for stakeholders, sponsors, and so on.

✔ Removes the onus from the consultant to prove something.

✔ Demonstrates dramatic ROI.

✔ Prompts requests for further partnering.

> Focus on output, not input, and value not price. If you're discussing price (be it cost, or effort, or resource commitment, or whatever) prior to conceptual agreement, then you've lost control of the discussion.

People ask me all the time what consulting model I use, as if consulting were a six-step dance that anyone could learn to lead. Consulting is actually a process that brings a myriad of models into play as needed. (Sometimes you may need coaching or survey models; other times you won't.) But there is a key and core process, and that is conceptual agreement.

The quicksand that all consultants skirt is the emphasis on deliverables. Consultants have been so successful in miseducating buyers about deliverables that now even buyers ask, "What are the deliverables?" What they are is worthless.

Deliverables are essentially low value, because they are commodities—workshops, interviews, procedural guides, and so forth—and are seldom directly held accountable for business results. Internal staffs are often trusted to create sales manuals while the actual development of the sales force is entrusted to outsiders. Buyers who demand deliverables are generally those who don't know what they don't know—that is, they have no idea what they're trying to achieve, only a notion of what they want to *do*; they don't know what the outputs should be, only what the inputs *should look like*.

> **Case Study**
>
> Early in my consulting career I visited the director of training at a large New York-based insurance company. He kept asking me what our training programs would cost. "Aren't you interested in finding out what they'll *deliver*?" I naively asked.
>
> "Look," he said, exasperated, "we have 2,000 managers and supervisors, and budget for about 20 courses of one kind or another. The more of those managers who go through most of those courses, the more successful I am. It's like getting all their tickets punched."
>
> That's when I realized that I either had to get out of the training business or had to stop dealing with idiots. I eventually did both.

Conceptual agreement is virtually impossible to obtain without the trust we've spoken about earlier. But internal consultants have a tremendous advantage in that they can be building that trust on an on-going basis, without pressure, and within a common cultural context. We external people are forced to try to build relationships during limited exposure to the buyer and with the pressure of a potential project on the line.

Yet, inexplicably, internal people don't take advantage of this significant leverage.

> Internal consultants and external consultants each have unique and intrinsic advantages, and are about equally endowed in that regard. But internal consultants tend to ignore, forsake, or destroy many of their advantages, leaving external consultants in relatively far stronger competitive positions.

Finally, if you can garner conceptual agreement with an economic buyer, there is no need for massive data gathering. Consultants of all stripes tend to engage in largely wasteful and inaccurate "needs analysis" and data consumption because they feel they need to justify their approaches and fees. They take the onus on themselves to prove that they're worth it.

Few needs analyses I've ever seen significantly increased either knowledge (let alone wisdom) or value.

Conceptual agreement with the buyer removes the onus on the consultant to be the expert and to prove his or her worth. It effectively demands that the buyer delineate the desired outcomes, develop the measures of success, and describe the value that will accrue to the organization as a result. Hence, conceptual agreement is the mechanism that generates true partnering, and prevents the hero role and all it demands, of the consultant (which is usually the goat role if anything goes astray).

No consulting project should proceed without obtaining conceptual agreement with the buyer, period. Ironically, one of the best ways to guarantee that is to confront, question, and resist the buyer—what I call "pushback."

PUSHING BACK

"Pushing back" means resisting the urge to go along with everything the buyer says, from the nature of the project, to the solution, to the best television shows. The reasons are both perceptual and pragmatic:

- ✔ The appearance of a yes man mentality both undermines credibility and does not serve your client well.
- ✔ All clients know what they want but few know what they need, which is why a professional is required for the analysis and intervention.
- ✔ Even if suggestions are not accepted, you prove your value in offering differing views and innovation.
- ✔ The worth of an outsider is new perspective and energy.

✔ Most clients are so immersed in their own operations that they usually fail to see even the obvious, let alone the subtle.

Pushback can range, depending on your degree of comfort (and chutzpah) along the continuum shown in Figure 4.4.

1. Targeted questioning. You ask the client to validate his or her beliefs and premises. (Never accept an nonvalidated premise,

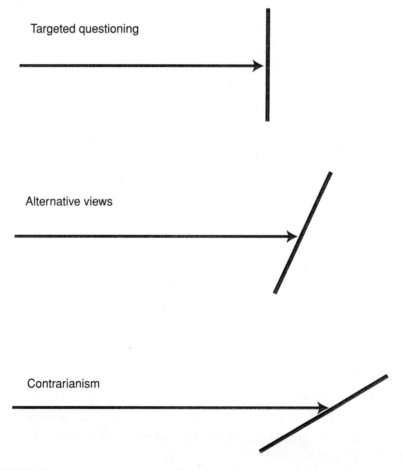

FIGURE 4.4 Increasing levels of pushback

that is, "We're losing clients because our technological infra-structure isn't supportive of their needs.") Examples of targeted questions:

- ✔ Why do you say that?
- ✔ What is the evidence for that statement?
- ✔ What have you actually observed?
- ✔ Who says this and why do you believe them?
- ✔ What independent validation do you have?
- ✔ Is this supported by actual experience?

Targeted questioning is conversational and collegial. The questions can be positioned from the standpoint of education and curiosity, but never cynicism or disbelief.

In opposing a preestablished point of view, you both establish credibility and serve the client well. This is a win/win maneuver, though not for the faint of heart.

2. Alternative views. In this position, the pushback is slightly stronger. If the client says, for example, "It's just impossible to get decent talent in this labor pool," instead of responding, "Why do you say that?" (targeted question) you might reply, "There are several schools of thought about that, one of which might apply to our situation: There's a need to take exceptional and heroic actions to attract the talent needed."

Statements that pose alternative views might include:

- ✔ That's not what turned out to be the cause the last time.
- ✔ In our industry, there have been several other reasons.
- ✔ The current literature suggests that the solution must be multifaceted.

✔ In my prior position (or on another project) we took a slightly different approach, which was very successful.

✔ What you're saying makes sense, but it's not the same resolution I've heard from others, which also makes sense.

✔ Is this what you'd recommend if you were in the customer's position, because I wonder what the customers would think about this proposal.

Alternative views inform the client that there are other perspectives and possibilities, but never that the client is *wrong* and you are *right*. It's a matter of re-opening evaluations, and removing blinders.

3. Contrarianism.[2] This is by far my favorite pushback mechanism, though it does fall into the categories of prudent risk, and no risk, no reward.

In contrarianism you oppose the client's position or plan. This will immediately rivet attention on you providing you with the chance to shine (or fry). But I like the odds.

You tell the client that the path suggested is not only inappropriate, but perhaps directly the opposite of what should be done. This prevents people from jumping on bandwagons or merely joining in the latest fads. ("Let's get that open meeting stuff in here!")

Examples would include:

✔ We shouldn't do that. That course failed miserably every time we've tried it in other departments.

✔ That's exactly why we shouldn't do it. Being popular isn't the point here; being accurate and honest is.

✔ Have you examined the risks? I have, and they are overwhelming, even if we succeed in the implementation.

---

[2]One of the brands I've established has actually been The Contrarian, which has stood me in good stead—and far apart from the crowd—over the years.

✔ Our clients are doing just the opposite, and this puts us not only at odds with them but with industry practices.

✔ No one will support this, no matter what they tell you.

✔ People are advocating you do this because they want it—and you—to fail. Don't go along with that plan.

Contrarianism is a sound position for a true peer, who isn't opposing the client viscerally, but who realizes that the client needs to make a 180° turn if he or she is to be successful.

> Contrarianism can create an internal brand, in that some clients will request the consultant whom they know won't go along just to be with the in-crowd and whose endorsement means that the path chosen must be objectively sound.

Ultimately, pushback is far less risky than robotic adherence and obsequious agreement. The danger of annoying a key buyer is far outweighed by the advantage of being considered a learned, objective, and—yes—fearless peer. True colleagues never refrain from resisting something they deem inappropriate, no matter how close the relationship.

This all revolves around the trust issue that we raised earlier in this chapter. If the other person believes that you honestly have his or her best interests in mind, no matter how much you may be causing discomfort or even pain, your viewpoint will be honored and seriously considered.

That's what the best external consultants do to overcome the disadvantage of not being immersed in the culture, history, and environment. And that's what internal consultants should do to negate the advantage that we external consultants are exploiting.

Case Study

Clients tell me all the time that communications is a problem because it's the number one complaint on employee surveys. They want to develop communications strategies and programs. Usually, when implemented by the HR department, they don't work. And for good reason.

I tell clients that communications *should be* the number one complaint, and that in good companies it always is. This silences the room, and creates rapt attention.

"Look," I continue, "you want employees hungry for information and with an urgency to contribute and be heard. The real key here is to create alternative *listening* avenues, so that they are satisfied they can be heard, via focus groups, e-mail, faxes, hot lines, surveys, and so forth. Then you tell them, regularly and specifically, what you've heard and what, if anything, you intend to do. That will reconcile this issue."

"That's completely counterintuitive!" someone will point out.

"Yes, and what's your point?" I reply.

I can be constructively and effectively contrarian about at least 50 percent of all traditional management concerns, from quality (you can have too much) to turnover (you can have too little).

SUGGESTED READING

Debunking the Designated Decoy by Russell J. White (Trenholm Publishing, 1998). This is a clever, self-published book the author sent me describing how to listen for real issues, avoid the decoys that are floated, and generally seek truth, justice, and the American Way in an organizational setting.

Formulating
the Proposal

How to Ensure that
You and the Buyer Meet
Each Other's Expectations

SUMMATIONS, NOT EXPLORATIONS:
THE NINE STEPS TO IRRESISTIBLE PROPOSALS

Proposals are as necessary for internal consultants as external consultants. They serve to protect the client and the consultant. One of the grave vulnerabilities of internal change agents is that they too often function on the fly, drifting into and out of projects without defined boundaries, clear accountabilities, or acknowledged credit.

There's nothing magic about the word, only the concept. You can call these contracts, agreements, protocols, or anything else that suits both you and the buyer. But the key is to have written concurrence and a mutually-supported, formalized approach.

Proposals are *summations* and not *explorations*. That is, they summarize conceptual agreement (see Chapter 4) and are therefore the formalization of previously-reached understandings. Proposals should meet the following criteria:

Proposals Provide	*Proposals Do Not Provide*
✔ Summation of prior agreement.	✔ New objectives and alternatives.
✔ Mutual guarantees and protection.	✔ Unilateral protection.
✔ A template for the entire project.	✔ A filed form that isn't again used.
✔ Options from which the client chooses.	✔ A "take it or leave it" approach.
✔ Joint and shared peer accountabilities.	✔ Buyer superiority, no accountability.
✔ Clear engagement and disengagement.	✔ Vague and uncertain involvement.
✔ Parameters for the project.	✔ Negotiating positions.
✔ Need for explicit sign-off/ approval.	✔ Toe-in-the-water, pilots, tests.
✔ Specific, situational responsiveness.	✔ Generic, off-the-shelf response.
✔ Means to enforce accountability.	✔ Reason to avoid accountability.

> No major project should be undertaken without a written, signed proposal. Buyers routinely expect this from external consultants, obviously for good reason. Why wouldn't they expect this from internal consultants?

In my experience, any project—no matter what the size, nature, or scope—can be represented in a two- or three-page proposal. The steps I recommend (and I am successful with more than 80 percent of my proposals) are as follows, always assuming that you've reached conceptual agreement with the economic buyer.

1. Situation Appraisal. This is a brief description of the conditions that gave rise to the need for the project. "The sales division has been in existence for 12 years, and has recently expanded to telemarketing with the acquisition of the Melvin Company" is not a good situation statement, since it merely records historical fact. Better: "There is friction between the telemarketing and field sales forces, causing lost sales and unhappy customers. This must be resolved with zero customer disruption and maximum sales productivity gain."

2. Objectives. I recommend that these be listed as business outcome bulleted points:

- ✔ Increase first year hire retention.
- ✔ Decrease orientation time from three weeks to one.
- ✔ Accelerate new hire's first sale on average to within 90 days of hire.

3. Measures of Success. Again, bulleted points from earlier discussions:

- ✔ Weekly and monthly sales reports.
- ✔ Anecdotal reporting by sales district managers.
- ✔ Quarterly turnover reports and exit interviews.

4. Value to the Organization. This is the final aspect of conceptual agreement embodied in points 2, 3, and 4. Once more, a simple format:

- ✔ New hire acquisition costs decrease by 20 percent.
- ✔ Turnover costs decrease by 50 percent.
- ✔ Morale and self-worth achieved earlier by new hires in tough areas.

5. Methodology and Options. More about this later in this chapter, but here is where you present the various alternatives that will meet the objectives, each with slightly higher value, albeit increased investment and commitment. These descriptions should be brief and the methodology is the least important aspect (something that human resources people find hard to embrace).

Option 1: We will create an employee hot line to gather anonymous reactions to the new compensation system, indications of true inequities, and other resistance not previously anticipated. We will develop patterns and strength of feedback, and provide weekly reports to you with suggestions for both how to acknowledge the response, and how to analyze and take actions on valid concerns.

> A clear, coherent, succinct proposal tells the buyer that you are a professional partner, concerned with his or her best interests, and that you are pragmatically and realistically attacking the key issues.

6. Timing. The approximate engagement point (e.g., "upon your acceptance" or "on March 1 as we discussed") and disengagement point (e.g., "about three months for option 1 from commencement").

7. Joint Accountabilities. We'll cover this in more depth later in this chapter, but this is a list of what you are individually and jointly responsible for:

- ✔ I will schedule, arrange, facilitate, and report on all focus groups.
- ✔ You will provide access to all of your direct reports.
- ✔ We will meet every second Friday morning to review progress.

8. Terms and Conditions. You might want to soften this to some-thing like "logistics and commitments" but the point is to make clear the investment relative to the returns just mentioned.

You should include here:

✔ Any financial outlays, purchases, investments, and so on.

✔ Time requirements.

✔ What abrogates the agreement (e.g., failure to provide key people, failure to act as a sponsor, inability to access key cus-tomers, etc.).

9. Acceptance. There should be a mutual sign-off, acknowledging this agreement to be accurate and binding. This is particularly vital for internal people who often take the blame for line managers' sloth, or who are thrust to low priority while still expected to deliver when con-sidered a high priority.

I've never understood why blasé internal change agents accept as-signments and projects without any official documentation or verifica-tion, when they are generally much more in need of it than are external people (whose clear fees exert pressure to both listen to us and to ac-cept our demands for support and partnership).

A proposal can't be submitted prior to conceptual agreement and can't be submitted to anyone other than the true, economic buyer. (They can be submitted, of course, under any conditions, but they will tend not to be accepted.)

While the creation of a proposal may seem threatening from the standpoint of time, politics, and hierarchy, it is actually the reverse: It will set you apart from the crowd, enable you to compete with external resources far more powerfully, and, most importantly, protect the qual-ity of the project for both the buyer and for you.

If a buyer doesn't want to take the time or trouble to provide you with the information needed and to consider a formal proposal, the buyer is either not serious or doesn't respect your efforts. The time to find out either issue is well before you begin the project.

PROVIDING VALUE-BASED OPTIONS

I've discovered few tools in the course of my career as powerful as providing options for prospects.

The core benefit is that the other person is subtly but effectively moved from "*Should* I do this?" to "*How* should I do this?" or to put it in a more personal way, from "*Should* I use Alan?" to "*How* should I use Alan?" This psychological shift includes these benefits:

✔ The issue is no longer you, but rather the project. Choices of implementation remove the onus from your shoulders about credibility and/or past history. You and the buyer immediately become partners in evaluating which alternatives would be the most appealing. This technique works particularly well with assertive, strong, decisive buyers who love to examine how fast and how thoroughly a project can be executed. It is freeing for a person to realize that his or her choices are not rigidly constrained but, instead, call for judgment to decide which may be best and under what conditions.

✔ The focus is not on the objective, but on which alternative makes the most sense. Once you have agreed on the objective, you're well on your way to conceptual agreement. Once it's even implicitly admitted that sales closing time must decrease, the choice of options to accomplish that end is generally harmonious and collegial. You can quickly move to measures and value and complete conceptual agreement.

> The offering of options I call the "choice of yeses," meaning that any option is positive for you. You are proceeding from "go/no go" to "go/go/go." This isn't a bad circumstance.

✔ There is an assumptive close that the project will proceed. This is one of the oldest and most clichéd devices in any sales tool kit, but that's because it works more often than not. It speeds along your sale and circumvents a buyer's potential need to involve others, obtain more feedback, and so forth.

✔ There is no interpersonal conflict involved in what the buyer wants to do versus what you want to do. If a buyer's premeditated solution makes sense to you, you can include it in the options. If it doesn't, you can at least provide options so that the buyer isn't confronted with "your idea that's better than his idea." (And you can always modify the buyer's options with the safeguards required within the context of these choices.

✔ The buyer tends to a larger commitment, since buyers are prone to escalate up the value chain, seeking greater benefit (even at greater investment).[1] Very few buyers pass up a chance to save money, but virtually none pass up the chance to increase value. This technique focuses the buyer on the value propositions of the various alternatives, which is precisely where the scrutiny should be, and not on the resource commitments (charge back, people, time, etc.). No buyer asks for a larger alternative than the ones offered. If you don't ask, you don't get.

✔ Buyers believe they get what they pay for. I call this The Mercedes-Benz Syndrome. A highly expensive car (or watch, or vacation, or suit) *must* be good. In fact, the buyer will take pains to support how good it is, because his or her ego is involved. "We took the high road here," and "We've made a major investment," and "We're going to do this the right way" are all phrases we hear from buyers who have made major investment decisions (and chosen more expensive options).

If you think about it, options like these work every day. Travel agents offer us alternative vacation packages to the exact same destination; auto dealers suggest an array of options and features for the same

---

[1]In employing options, I've noticed that buyers view increasing investment as arithmetic, but increasing value as exponential, thereby significantly increasing perceptions of ROI as value increases.

> No buyer states that she's proud to have found the cheapest way to motivate people, build relationships, respond to customers, or retain staff. She says, instead, "We will spare nothing to be the best that we can be. . . ." This is the ego state that options capitalize on.

basic transportation; computer hardware and software provide a dazzling array of capabilities and capacities merely to do word processing or create spreadsheets.

For example, if you're trying to nail down the buyer for a meeting, don't offer a specific date and time. Suggest this: "I'm available for

---

Case Study

On those infrequent but potentially serious occasions when I show up very late for my hotel reservation, and the desk clerk has said, "I'm sorry, we didn't think you were coming, and gave away the room," I've developed an ironclad choice of options to respond.

"Well, you always have suites available at all hours for VIPs; we know that." Or: "You could transport me at your expense to another, comparable hotel and put me up there, again at your expense." Or: "We could wake up the general manager and see what he has to say about this. Which do you prefer?"

The bewildered desk clerk will usually be speechless for 10 seconds, considering the lunatic who stands before her, and will then promptly offer a suite, since they are indeed available and are by far the least costly and least worrying outcome.

Who's crazy now?[2]

---

[2]I warn you only never to try this with a spouse or significant other over the long term. When my wife wants to know where we should go for dinner, and I say, "Well, we have some options," she simply says, "You're not dealing with a client now; pick a restaurant and make a reservation!"

lunch today, any time tomorrow morning, lunch tomorrow, or I can come in early the day after. What's best for your schedule?" (You can do the same with the buyer's secretary if you're trying to get time on the buyer's calendar.)

Another example: "I can e-mail you the proposal, FedEx it to your sales meeting, or stop by with it when you return. What's best for you?"

If you use the "choice of yeses" on a regular basis, I'll guarantee that you'll enjoy far greater success in most of your business dealings, not only in your consulting work. And there's one other variant of this that might be of interest.

I call this "not taking a no." Experience suggests that if someone tells you no you're unlikely to reverse that decision no matter how frequent, emotional, or desperate your appeals. In fact, the odds are probably 99:1 against a reversal. The psychological reason for this is that the other person's ego is closely tied to the decision, and to reverse it for no other reason than your insistence usually means a loss of face, bowing under pressure, and failing to stand up to one's beliefs. Those are daunting roadblocks.

However, *if you provide new information*, you change the odds perhaps as far as to 50:50. This is because you are saving the buyer's ego by adding information that was not known before, thereby providing a legitimate and rational reason to change one's earlier stance.

For example: "I don't think I've mentioned that we have only this limited window of opportunity, and if we don't act now, we can't try this again for nearly 12 months." Or: "I don't think I mentioned that this request was the first choice by far on the recent customer survey." Or: "I've just learned—and wanted to relay to you—that our competition has begun a similar initiative and the longer we wait, the more of a head start they will have."

You get the idea. Don't just accept a no, but don't try to reverse it by brute force or volume, either. Use the finesse of new information as you would a judo move, using the buyer's own momentum to change direction.

Practice these techniques diligently and you'll be known as a highly persuasive consultant. Teach them to your own clients, and you'll be known as a brilliant consultant.

> Seek to prevent a no by employing a "choice of yeses." Try to reverse a no by providing new information. If you learn to use these techniques smoothly and well, you will enjoy a dramatic success rate in creating and closing new assignments *on your terms.*

ESTABLISHING JOINT ACCOUNTABILITIES

There is a rather alarming school of thought among some people who have written on the subject of organizational consulting and internal consultants. They picture management as a monolithic, evil enemy, which will exhibit a tropism toward the harsh, inhumane, and impersonal. Therefore, management must be fought as a true adversary, and the point is to try to bring enlightenment to these corporate descendants of Ming the Merciless. Ironically, a great deal of this enlightenment is supposed to emanate from faddish approaches and jargon, as if rearranging the chairs in the room will shift power. (All it really does is cause a pain in the rear.)

Another philosophy, less alarming but no less jejune, contends that consultants *are* the change agents, responsible for implementing recommendations, and actually do something to the client. That's a pedestal that I don't ever want to ascend, because the only ensuing direction is downward. (They say it's never the fall that kills you, but rather the sudden stop.)

My belief and unqualified experience is that consulting is a team sport. We consultants *collaborate* with our line clients, and the buyer is our *partner.*

When a CFO barked at me during a meeting analyzing why more progress hadn't been achieved in our project, "What's wrong?! You're the change agent!" I responded, *"No, you're the major change agent,* and you haven't been supporting the initiative. What am I supposed to do, take over your job?"

There are some things only a consultant can credibly (or competently) do, and some things only the client (or other stakeholders) can do. Unless we all work in concert, neither believing that we're super-

Case Study

I was interviewing a woman for a top director of human resources position at a major corporation. Halfway through the interview I asked her if she had ever felt alone or isolated as the director of human resources in prior positions.

"Of course not," she coolly replied. "All managers are directors of human resources, so we're all in this together."

One of the great interview replies of all time. I think the same thing about consultants working to create change. We're all change agents, managers, and consultants, alike.

heroes helping the downtrodden nor soldiers fighting the enemy, not everything will get done. It's as simple as that.

The consultants who get it are those who view themselves as part of a healthy, synergistic effort with their clients. That means tucking away both paranoia and ego. I call this "post-heroic consulting."

Establishing joint accountabilities is a rational, objective, and transparent process that establishes (or formalizes) the partnership. Here is an idea of what each party can solely or at least best do on a generic basis:

Buyer

✔ Make resources available.
✔ Serve as exemplar or model.
✔ Enforce rewards and punishments.

Consultant

✔ Offer untainted views.
✔ Bring best practices from elsewhere.
✔ Confront the buyer.

Buyer	Consultant
✔ Enforce institutionalization.	✔ Conduct objective data gathering.
✔ Identify key sponsors/ stakeholders.	✔ Offer appropriate methodologies.
✔ Find funding.	✔ Train/develop client personnel.
✔ Compensate for project disruption.	✔ Determine how to minimize disruption.
✔ Request repeat/return engagements.	✔ Identify true support and resistance.

In addition, there are joint accountabilities that must be accepted by both parties, which may include:

- ✔ Notification of unexpected obstacles.
- ✔ Communication of status and progress regularly.
- ✔ Influencing and co-opting key supporters/resistors.
- ✔ Exploiting the victories and advantages.
- ✔ Quickly responding to problems.
- ✔ Conformance to terms and conditions agreed upon.

One of the chronic and avoidable failures of internal consulting projects is in the buyer's slothful position that the consultant is responsible for the project and that the buyer can simply get back to business as usual. This is why so many HR projects stumble before they leave the gate. The people in the trenches know as surely as a dog can find the scraps in the dishwasher that anything introduced as someone else's project need not be given hardy commitment. In fact, lip service compliance will serve just fine until the rapidly approaching day when the project collapses of its own (lack of) weight.

An external consultant can't accept the responsibility for most of the project's implementation, because he or she is simply not there, not on-site, not present in sufficient numbers. The fact that the internal consultant *is* there changes nothing—any project is the responsibility of both buyer and consultant, the latter providing the methodology and processes, but the former providing the resources and implementation.

There's another reason to vigorously formalize joint accountabilities and partnering, albeit mundane: If you get roped into doing the lion's share of the work,[3] you won't have time to do any other work. That is, you won't be in a position to take on other projects, conduct an appraisal of your own work, create a strategy for your department (or career), and, not incidentally, relax.

> In my busiest year, I handled 34 consulting projects, not all overlapping, but all within the year. Some were of a few weeks, some transcended the calendar year. Most were of several months. Not one client ever expressed concerns about being shortchanged, and I was not ground into dust by the experience. If I can do this working with a myriad of clients, internal consultants can certainly juggle a few projects at a time.

If you allow yourself to be enveloped by a project, you're actually cheating your clients, since you're not developing the breadth of experiences and best practices that actually constitute a major part of your value. The best internal consultants work cross-functionally, cross-culturally, and cross-hierarchically, and engage in several projects at once. (Lest you contend that you're lucky to be asked to work on even one project at a time, let me refer you back to the marketing aspects of this book. I've never seen any organization of any decent size without the need for ongoing consulting help in a variety of areas.)

To summarize: Joint accountabilities are an absolutely essential feature of the consulting process and deserve their own segment in the proposal. No matter how convivial or trusting the relationship with the buyer, accountabilities should be specified and formalized, which in turn reinforce the nature of the partnership. Properly es-

---

[3]Be aware that "lion's share" really denotes "all" not "most," and has only recently been bastardized into the latter meaning.

tablished, joint accountabilities will free your time for additional work and play.

But most of all, the success of a project *is not* based on the consultants' methodology or persuasive powers. It is based on the willingness, ability, and investment of the buyer and stakeholders to perpetuate and reinforce the desired changes. *They* are the true change agents in that regard. Consultants can recommend, design, and even introduce change, but only the client can accept, embrace, reinforce, and maintain change.

Before we leave the subject, let's examine how to contain the changes within a coherent framework and avoid confusion.

AVOIDING SCOPE CREEP

Scope creep occurs when the buyer (or others) continues to request additional tasks and deliverables ad infinitum, as if instead of committing to a project you've in fact sold your soul.

This is the La Brea tar pit of consulting. After a while you notice the bones of prehistoric consultants alongside and you realize there is no escape. The key is to avoid the tar pit, because you can never extricate yourself from it.

On an internal basis, consultants who fall prey to scope creep can become de facto members of the client organization. That may seem like a good thing at first, especially if one is assigned to support that unit. But in actuality, it means that the consultants' independence, objectivity, and credibility have been co-opted and negated. And that's a serious price to pay for acceptance.

> Scope creep is pernicious because it is usually not done with malice aforethought. The client isn't nefariously planning to take advantage of the consultant, but actually seems to be showing appreciation for the consultant, and therein is the danger.

> ### Case Study
>
> When I worked with the Hewlett-Packard consulting arm, one of the major problems was diminishing and even disappearing margins. HP had determined that their implementation people were randomly and frequently committing to undocumented promises.
>
> "Undocumented promises," a fabulous bureaucratic phrase, simply meant that the implementation people—each working on a small part of an overall several million dollar project—were afraid of jeopardizing the project (and drawing attention to themselves) by denying the client any request. And that meant, incredibly, *any* member of the client, and *any* request, no matter how bizarre or remote from the client. Some even wound up writing code or fixing software that the client had had trouble with for years in completely divorced areas.
>
> The result of not jeopardizing the project was to sink the project for HP, since all the extra work far exceeded the proposal estimates, and the profit margin declined to near-zero. Ergo, the hazards of scope creep.

Irrelevant requests may come from the buyer, which is bad enough, but they can also come from others in the buyer's organization who may be looking for free help, trying to exert leverage and power, or simply under the impression that you're all part of the same family. When you begin fulfilling requests from anyone who asks, you're being subsumed by scope creep.

It usually occurs because of one or more of these reasons. You can see by their number that scope creep is a slippery slope:

- ✔ Objectives for the project aren't clear.
- ✔ Legitimate tangential requests turn into peripheral demands from the tangential requests.
- ✔ The buyer is impressed by your work and wants to apply it elsewhere.

✔ The buyer is shorthanded and sees any warm body as potential help to stave off the deluge.

✔ The consultant's self-esteem is low and the reaction is to try to continually prove oneself.

✔ The hierarchy of the organization has taken precedence over the peer relationship of consulting partnerships and the consultant is afraid to say no.

✔ The project has failed or is dead and no one knows it or admits to it.

✔ Measure devices for the project aren't clear, so it's hard or impossible to tell whether the project is complete.

✔ There is no disengagement mechanism, or the consultant doesn't know how to employ it, or the buyer ignores it.

✔ You are in a relationship that is more of a *retainer* relationship than a *project* relationship.

There is a huge difference between a project relationship and a client simply having access to your smarts. Differentiate between these two as soon as you recognize the indicators.

No wonder it's so simple to become entrapped by scope creep. The prevention is far more effective than the contingencies to escape it (and far less bruising to the body and ego), but let's take a look at both, from the ridiculous to the sublime.

Avoiding the Agony of Scope Creep

1. Retainer vs. project. Most internal consultants never make this differentiation. A project involves formal objectives, measures, and so forth (as set forth in the proposal discussed earlier) and has clear starting and ending points. Retainers mean that the client merely needs access to your wisdom and com-

petence, and you serve as a sounding board, advisor, coach, or mentor, *but you do not take on specific project work.* For those of you who support discrete departments or functions, you are continually on retainer for your client, but you shouldn't confuse that with additionally taking on whatever specific projects the client casually requests. Ensure that the buyer understands the distinction. Otherwise, you're just another hired hand.

2. Clear objectives and tight measurement. The tighter the objectives, the more difficult for the scope to creep. Think of the objectives as crisp, strong walls, and not porous, weak boundaries. (See Figure 5.1.)

   Increasingly crisp (and bounded) objectives would be:

   ✔ Improve morale.
   ✔ Improve the poor morale causing high attrition rates.
   ✔ Reduce attrition in the sales force.
   ✔ Reduce attrition in the sales force to industry average or below.

   The final example is a discernible business outcome (and morale may or may not be causal). It's easily measurable.

3. Disengagement mechanisms. A project ceases when the objectives are met, which should be within the time frames specified. If a project is completed earlier than the estimate, it's

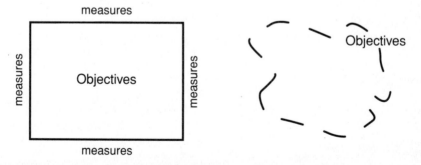

FIGURE 5.1 Clear vs. porous measures based on clear objectives

over and the client doesn't own you until the original completion date. If the project isn't completed on time, then the meeting of the objectives is reason to extend the commitment dates, of course. But there must be agreement that the project is over upon completion[4] and typical disengagement mechanisms are final reports, final management briefings, delivery of the hardware/software/manuals, process implemented among line managers and in use, and so on.

4. Don't beat a dead horse (and never attempt to ride one). Some projects fail. Welcome to my world. Don't throw good money after bad by trying to steer the *Titanic*. Admit the failure, affix cause (never blame, unless it's your own), learn, and move on. If you continue to try to revive a hopeless project, you'll be engaged in fatal scope creep—not for the client or the project, but for your career. Tuck your ego away.

> If you've never been part of a failed project, you're just not trying. That is, you haven't attempted innovative, daring, and high impact consulting.

5. Believe in yourself and your role.   You're a peer of the buyer, and you assist the buyer best when you oppose the buyer at appropriate times. Value what you do and what you represent, and you'll be able to resist the buyer's inadvertent or advertent attempts to shanghai you into impressed labor. If it helps, engage in exercises with your colleagues to establish a better self-image. (Ironically, many internal consultants need external consultants to help them master this process, and I'm not being sarcastic. External consultants—at least good ones—use other consultants all the time, and consulting firms have been among my largest clients.)

---

[4]Or, gasp, admission of failure!

6. Just say no.   Explain politely to anyone who asks that the request isn't fair to the buyer, since it will consume your time and energy and distract from the buyer's objectives. Scope creep *cannot occur* if you say no often enough.

   Focus on your client's objectives, and you'll avoid the tar pits. Consultants should be smarter than the dinosaurs.

SUGGESTED READING

How to Write A Proposal That's Accepted Every Time by Alan Weiss (Kennedy Information, 1999). Unabashedly, I believe my book is simply the best and is in use by many consulting organizations and thousands of consultants. It includes a CD ROM with examples of large and small proposals, how to present them, how to follow up, and how to gain conceptual agreement through conversational questioning.

Chapter 6

The Value Proposition

Why Every Client Knows What's Wanted but Not Necessarily What's Needed

THE DIFFERENCE BETWEEN "FIX" AND "IMPROVE"

There are two dimensions of value that consultants bring to a client engagement. The obvious one is the value attendant to completing the project and meeting the client's objectives, which we focused on in Chapter 4.

The second is the inherent value that we bring as the interventionists. If we don't possess and *demonstrably convey* a unique value proposition of our own, then the project's value can be generated by virtually anyone. We've become undifferentiated commodities, with one alternative as good as another.[1]

---

[1] In fact, Victor Vroom of Yale University, a long-time expert on leadership and decision theory, calls a decision "low quality" when any one alternative is as good as another in the decision maker's view. See his book, with Philip Yetton, *Leadership and Decision Making*, University of Pittsburgh Press, 1973.

If you'd ever like to test your unique value proposition to your prospective client, ask these three questions:

- ✔ Why me?
- ✔ Why now?
- ✔ Why in this manner?

Why Me? What distinguishing traits, experiences, values, relationships, skills, behaviors, credentials, and other singular combinations of traits do you bring to the table that create an advantage for the client? You should be able to readily generate such a list and not assume that the buyer can divine all your assets through osmosis. If you can't generate such a list yourself, then you need development in the categories listed (e.g., further line experience, skills in conflict resolution, an M.B.A.), which is why a career in HR is not a positive distinguishing trait but rather tends to be a constraining one.

Why Now? Is there a window of opportunity that will disappear? Is there some event occurring or anticipated that drives the urgency? What will happen if nothing at all is done? What's the trend? The greater the impetus for action as a result of these factors, the more value your rapid intervention can provide. (It's fascinating that internal people are much better able to respond to time-critical demands, yet the clients still expend the time to find and engage external consultants so often.)

Why in This Manner? Why utilize consulting help at all? Has this been tried before and gone haywire? Is there a particular need for objective involvement outside the area? Is there precedent, or is

---

If you don't bring additional and discernible value to a project, then you're only as good as the next person. But if you bring clear value-added, then you become an integral and perhaps irreplaceable aspect of the solution or improvement.

this unprecedented? Knowing the reasons for the request—or for entertaining your proactive suggestions—also helps to calibrate the value proposition.

One of the most important inherent aspects of a unique value proposition is the ability to proactively suggest improvement, and not merely respond to appeals to fix something. This is an implicit advantage for internal consultants over external consultants, but one not utilized nearly enough. After all, who is in a better position to observe what seem to be adequate operations and suggest further ways to improve performance and standards? There's no way an external resource can do that.

Moreover, even when called upon to solve a problem, there is the opportunity for an internal person to instead suggest raising the bar. *Every client I've ever met knows exactly what they want. But few know what they really* **need**. *The difference between what they think they want and what they really need is our value-added.*

Internal people are forever sitting around waiting for an alarm to sound, a customer to squawk, or the roof to fall in. They spend far too little time helping to establish preventive actions, anticipate demand, explore further improvements, and establish best practices. Yet there is far more value in raising the bar than there is in merely restoring performance to past levels after a decline.

Figure 6.1 shows the difference between simply restorative actions and true breakthrough actions.

Problem solving is a commodity, and today as testimony to that fact, is often done by most frequently asked questions on web sites, automated phone menus, and manuals that diagnose problems on flow charts. But innovation is a distinct and clear benefit, requiring new thinking, novel interventions, and—gasp—risk.

Perhaps there is no greater factor repressing internal consultants than the fear of risk and failure. External consultants are willing to accept prudent risk in return for dramatic improvements. After all, our retirement plans, bonuses, and collegial relationships aren't with our client companies. But internal people would seem to have so much at risk that problem solving is attractive—removing the pain, assuaging the hurt, eliminating the annoyance—while innovation involves prohibitive risk—disruption, violating the not broke/don't fix rubric, moving into areas without precedent.

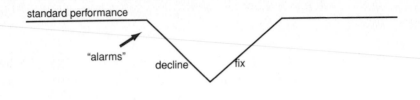

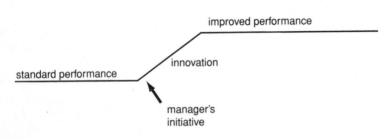

FIGURE 6.1   Problem solving vs. innovation

Yet risk taking is what proactive leadership is all about, and if internal consultants aren't known for it (remember the why me/now/manner questions), then that help will be drawn into the innovation vacuum from elsewhere.

You should be spending your time every day—something that

If you're not going to take risks or make proactive suggestions, and simply sit by the phone waiting to be called, you're not a consultant, but a management repair person, no different from an electrician, except that you're not even sure where the wiring leads.

external consultants cannot do within the prospect—asking these questions:

✔ Where are we complacent and uncritical of our performance?

✔ In what areas do we lead *where we can further increase the gap?*

✔ What is key to our strategy that hasn't been improved recently?

✔ Where have people and processes been in place with greatest longevity?

✔ Where is a good pilot area to demonstrate ongoing improvement?

✔ Where is most problem solving now occurring (and, hence, bandages are being applied in place of real improvement)?

No risk, no reward (or, as William Penn observed, "No cross, no crown"). If you need to, utilize a simple risk/reward instrument to help your client (and yourself) visualize the potential upside and manage prudent risk.

In Figure 6.2 you see one such simple approach.[2] You can use your own scale of risk, but my criteria are:

✔ Anything that is +3 to +5 with a downside of −1 to −2 should be pursued.

✔ Anything of +2 to +3 with 0 or −1 risk should be pursued.

✔ Anything of +4 to +5 risk should be avoided unless you can clearly demonstrate how to avoid and/or control the risk.

✔ Generally, reward should outperform risk by a factor of 2.

Use your own and your culture's risk orientation (e.g., this will be higher in advertising and lower in banking) but use something to demonstrate the wisdom of seeking improvement and the intelligent assessment of risk.

---

[2]This originally appeared in *The Innovation Formula: How Organizations Turn Change Into Opportunity*, by Mike Robert and Alan Weiss (Harper & Row, 1988).

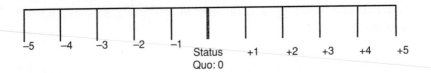

Question: What is the best and worst that might result?

+5 = Paradigm-breaking improvement, industry leader.
+4 = Dramatic improvement, major publicity.
+3 = Strong benefits, organization-wide.
+2 = Minor benefits, localized.
+1 = Very minor improvement, barely noticed.

−1 = Very minor setback, barely noticed.
−2 = Minor setback, controlled locally.
−3 = Public setback, requires damage control.
−4 = Major defeat, financial damages, recovery time needed.
−5 = Devastating losses.

FIGURE 6.2 Risk/reward ratio

If you can make this case articulately and methodically, you can foster innovation in any environment and be a hero for doing so. The greatest risk of all—for you as a consultant and for the organization—is to risk nothing and gain nothing over protracted periods.

THE DIFFERENCE BETWEEN INPUT AND OUTPUT

One of the greatest lessons I've learned in the consulting trade is the difference between input and output. Another way to view this is the difference between tasks and results. In my book, "deliverables" are tasks, and that simplifies things nicely.

The only true value is the value of changed, improved, or somehow altered results. We are in business to improve the client's condition, and that improvement must be manifest. That's why objectives that include things such as "greater clarity," "better understanding," "a heightened awareness," and other such evanescent events are largely worthless.

Attitude, learning, skills, and everything else that can be improved without a demonstrable business result are simply not very valuable. It's like the salesperson who improves call rates from 8 per day to 30 per day without increasing sales. (Or, as wit Dorothy Parker once observed, "Is it really progress if we teach a cannibal to use a fork?")

But not far behind are the reports, classes, audits, installations, manuals, and other consulting esoterica that are merely means to an end. One of the most horrid aspects of the vaunted—and hugely expensive—quality efforts of the 1980s and 1990s was that a significant percentage of improvements never reached the customer, and like the tired tree forever falling in the forest, there was no sound. (In fact, in many cases, quality simply was an effort to win an award and not win over a customer.)

Here's how we have to view our craft and our client relationships (Figure 6.3).

In Figure 6.3, the first column represents those skills, experiences, traits, and blessing that may constitute our current value propo-

Consultant's Past	Competency/Methodology	Client's Future
• Experiences.	• Obversation.	• Larger sales.
• Education.	• Workshops.	• Higher retention.
• Victories and defeats.	• Facilitation.	• Lower attrition.
• Travel.	• Coaching.	• Reduced stress.
• Socialization.	• Manuals.	• Better communication.
• Collaborations.	• Training.	• Faster responsiveness.
• Problem solving.	• Focus groups.	• Larger market share.
• Decision making.	• Systems and procedures.	• Enhanced image.
• Planning.	• Conflict resolution.	• Greater safety.
• Innovation.	• Negotiating.	• Higher quality.
• Etc.	• Confrontation.	• Reduced expenses.
	• Etc.	• Etc.
Consultant/raw material	Consultant transfer mechanism	Client results

FIGURE 6.3 Consultant's past becoming client's future

sition. These differ for all of us, meaning that unique combinations are not that difficult to create.

In the second column is a representation of the interventions and methodologies that we may employ. These, too, will grow and evolve (if we're any good), and add to our value proposition.

But the third column is the real power for the client. Those are the results—the outputs—that our background and interventions can generate. *The problem with internal consultants is that they tend to focus on the first two columns and place value on them when, in fact, the value is on the third.*

Consequently, the courses we're certified to teach, the instruments we use from vendors, the finely-honed focus group or workshop are relatively inconsequential without the third column, and it's upon that column that value should be based. In other words, as an external consultant charging a fee, my fee is based on the third-column results, not middle delivery or first-column credentials. Though these two elements may constitute my unique value as to *why I should be awarded the project,* they don't represent the final worth of the project.

Unless you can create the third column for your client, you can never really establish the true value of the project for the buyer. And that's a shame, because that's the lingering and annualized true value. This is why silly HR concepts such as "four levels" of measurement are never used by competent external consultants and never accepted by powerful buyers. Knowledge change, attitude change, learning improvement, and similar factors are unimportant *unless actual business results are changed.* And those results don't have to be sublime, such as greater market share and higher retention, although those are terrific outputs. They can include improved teamwork, faster conflict resolution, and more rapid information exchange—so long as they are connected to a business outcome (e.g., faster information exchange

> Practice turning any job into outputs, but most of all practice with your own job. Are you focused on the input and methodology, or on the outputs and results? If you manage people, how are you evaluating their work and progress?

between customer service and field reps will result in delivery delays being resolved on the spot by the key client contact).

I can change virtually any job responsibility from an input to an output. The salesperson who says her job is to make sales calls must understand that the job is actually to bring in new business. The assistant who says the job is to answer the phone must be re-educated to believe that it's actually about directing inquiries to the proper destination for resolution.

What are you doing to create such re-education? What is your own philosophy? Here's an exercise that can be quite useful, but also somewhat painful. (If you manage others, it's very helpful to do this as a team.)

In the first column, write the areas for which you will be evaluated at the next planned evaluation session. In the second column, write the percentage of your evaluation based on this criterion. In the third column, write the amount of time you currently spend on that evaluation area in a typical week. In the final column, express that evaluation area as a business result or output. If it already is one in your judgment, then just carry the wording over.

Evaluation Area	Weight	Time Spent	Output Conversion
_____	_____	_____	_____
_____	_____	_____	_____
_____	_____	_____	_____
_____	_____	_____	_____
_____	_____	_____	_____
_____	_____	_____	_____

What total evaluation weight and how much time is being spent on input rather than output? In other words, if the evaluation area is "Make two visits a quarter to all four field offices" and the conversion you made was "Build field office self-sufficiency in handling customer complaints locally," you're being evaluated on the input, not the result. If the evaluation area is "Design and conduct a workshop on sales closing techniques" and the conversion is "Reduce field closing time" you're also on the input side. But if the evaluation area is "Reduce attrition in the call center so that customer waiting time is reduced," and you feel (rightly) that you have an output already in that goal, then you're in business.

> Input versus output is a simple concept, but then consulting is mostly about the application of common sense. If you can master this with prospective clients and in managing your own approach, you will be in rarefied air, and much more competitive with outside resources.

I can make a case that most of our lives should be about output, not input. That's not to say that tasks and approaches aren't important for reaching the goal. But I am saying that people are relieved to say that the fire is out, and not that the sprinkler system operated at 150 pounds per square inch, and that the organization's tough growth goals were met, and not that the new sales manual looks fabulous in its four color binder.

The next time you're devising smile sheets to applaud yourself on how well a group loved your workshop, consider instead asking their managers in 60 days whether they have improved their performances on the job. That's a lot more critical, a lot more threatening, and a lot more valuable. I've never been paid a lot of money to have people like me. As one client pointed out, "I don't care if everyone here hates you by the time you're done, as long as they've learned how to cut delivery time by at least 25 percent so we're competitive in that area."

ASKING THE "WHY" QUESTION

A woman told me the other day that she was shocked that I could make so much money for providing nothing more than common sense.

I told her that I was, too.

Yet common sense is in too short supply. That's why you find executives spending a fortune to find out what people on the front line

---

Case Study

In March 2002, Shaw's Supermarkets in Rhode Island discovered more than $40 million in inventory losses. That fact alone just about boggles the mind. You have to work hard or be creatively stupid to miss $40 million in inventory.

But the lunacy was just beginning.

In reaction, Shaw's issued a letter to all employees telling them that they were likely to be searched at any time and refusing to be searched would constitute grounds for dismissal.

"Where are the human resources people," I asked my wife, "who should be advising the CEO that this is madness?"

Then we learned that the vice president of human resources (along with the vice president of operations) had signed the letter! The next day, after 24 hours of execrable public relations and lead stories on every news show, the CEO apologized, called the letter unauthorized, and explained that he had never been told and would have never agreed to it.

Everyone went back to work. Unfortunately, that included the vice president of human resources.

---

know like the backs of their hands, and why policies are created that actually negate each other. Bureaucracy and common sense are not bedfellows, strange or otherwise.

All that anyone had to ask is, "Why are we doing this?" Here are the possible answers and analyses of those responses.

"Why are we considering sending this letter to employees?"

✔ Because we have to stop these huge inventory losses.

But why do you think that it's employee theft? Do you have any evidence? Have you considered the adverse morale and publicity that will result from such a letter?

✔ Because we suspect employees are stealing.

Then at least find some evidence that supports your case about those you suspect, and leave the other 99.9 percent alone.

✔ Because we have evidence of some employees stealing.

Then prosecute them publicly and send that message to everyone.

✔ Because we're not sure what caused the losses and we intend to attack every possibility.

Does that include aliens and Bill Gates? There are consequences to every action, and the consequences here outweigh the advantages. Don't forget, we have a union and customers who are sympathetic to the workers.

Internal consultants get whacked with fait accompli more often than external people. That's because they don't ask why as often, and a vicious cycle ensues (see Figure 6.4).

> We always ask how, seldom ask what, and virtually never ask why. You can be a hero without any kind of methodology at all merely by helping the client understand why and evaluating whether the how will justify the why.

Some years ago a consulting firm I worked for—full of consultants, but all internal to our own organization, though external to our clients—decided that it would dramatically hype sales in a tough year if the top three producers received new Cadillac El Dorados. It was decided that competition for just the three top spots would vastly increase the productivity of all 25 salespeople.

We never asked why we were doing this. The answer was to improve profits. That means that performance over the prior year would have to improve, meaning that only incentives *that were based on individual improvement over that person's prior year* would do any good.

Instead, in our firm the same three top producers of the prior year finished in those spots in the Caddy year, meaning that we had the exact same performance, minus the $60,000 cost of the three cars, meaning we took a $60,000 hit against our margins!

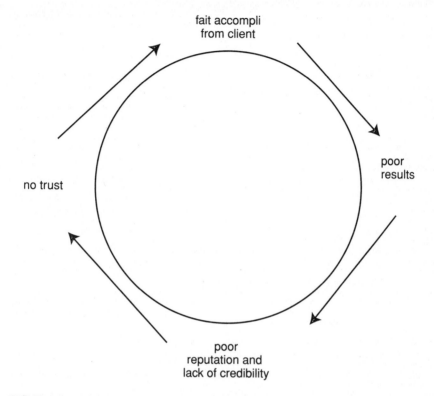

FIGURE 6.4 The consultant fait accompli vicious cycle

There are ways to ask why successfully and ways to end your career with it. "Why on earth are you thinking of doing *that*?" is not the way to approach a senior vice president. But "As part of my background information I always want to know why we've decided to do this at the current time with these resources" is a solid, objective inquiry.

Not asking why is endemic and catastrophic.

Asking why is actually a device to compare the alternative chosen (the fait accompli in many cases) to the objectives that are to be met. In so doing, you may discover any of the following dynamics, all of which will make you an effective and highly regarded resource.

✔ There are no objectives. An alternative was simply propped up and received support, despite the fact that it represented means without ends. For example, *why* institute a dress down Friday, or change the parking configuration? In many cases, it's just because someone thought it might be a good idea, has a personal agenda, or is trying to be popular—all terrible reasons for change.

✔ There is a legitimate objective (the "what") but only a single alternative (the "how") has been considered. It may be someone's pet choice, or a default position, or merely habit. But it's always valuable to generate other alternatives for comparison's sake. (One of my clients, when forced to do this on the eve of automatically renewing its rental car corporate contract, actually discovered that it was cheaper for its salespeople to take cabs and limos, and saved tens of thousands of dollars by abandoning the default alternative.)

✔ The buyer is using faulty data, poor assumptions, or marred basic premises to make the decision (e.g., we have missing inventory because our employees are thieves). This is the organizational morass of throwing good money after bad. You, therefore, have the opportunity to stanch the flow. (See the final section in this chapter.)

✔ No one knows why. Your client has also been handed a fait accompli in the form of a delayed project, a vague memo from the boss, or an assumption that something needs to be done some place in some way. I once found that a triplicate copy of every transaction in a compensation area of Prudential Insurance was being sent to the Scranton Files. No one knew what that area was or why it needed that copy. I found out that they were abandoned mine shafts, purchased in the 1950s outside Scranton, Pennsylvania, to be used to store hard copies in the event that nuclear war destroyed all other records. We stopped sending the copies one morning and no one ever complained. We saved thousands, though we ended a tradition.

✔ Someone has ordered something and that person is far removed from the actual facts. This was the story of the charge of the Light Brigade, when an heroic charge into machine guns and cannon was obliterated. The charge should never have taken place, but Lord Raglan never bothered to check because he wanted to yell, "Charge!" so much. Gettysburg was the same way. The corporate battlefield is littered with the fallen consultants who refused to stand up and say, "This way lies doom!"

Doctors agree to the value "First, do no harm." Consultants need to adhere to the value "First, permit no harm." It's our sacred duty to head off the nonsensical, prevent the reprehensible, and stop the madness.

That sounds tough. But you really only need ask, "Why?"

CONFRONTING BASIC PREMISES

Organizations hold a variety of beliefs near and dear. These may be business philosophies ("The customer is always right"), cultural paradigms ("No one ever got into trouble in accounting by turning down expense requests"), or accountability constraints ("If you want to work in sales, be prepared to give up your home life"). Some are dead-on accurate, some are situational, some are largely myth, and some are outright falsehoods.

But the absolute fact is that they will, indeed, be across the board, meaning that you can bet your next paycheck that a significant number of corporate premises will not be totally accurate. And the problem, of course, is that internal people are often caught up in them, part of them, or perpetrators of them! External people have no such problem and are usually aghast at what their clients purport to be true.

Corporate mythology can transmogrify anything. The best advice is to always ask, "What's our evidence for this belief?" You'll find that it's often nothing more than one person's opinion or some anecdote handed down from a lost source.

Confront directly any premise you hear that is not backed up by evidence, examples of which may include:

- ✔ We should be able to grow in Europe by 10 percent next year.
- ✔ We have a productivity problem in manufacturing.
- ✔ Temporary hires will not show the same dedication as full-timers.
- ✔ We're below the industry average on turnover.
- ✔ Our customers prefer an automated response system.
- ✔ The compensation system is actually depressing growth.

If you do this *immediately* upon hearing the potentially faulty premise, you prevent an entire project or initiative from being launched on a leaky hull. If you wait, your passivity will have indicated agreement with the premise and you will have missed an opportunity to provide tremendous value early. ("Why bring this up now? Why didn't you mention it when we first created plans for the new system?")

I'm not implying that most poor premises are malicious or deliberately parochial (though surely a minority is). I am suggesting that no matter how innocent the rationale, the resultant effect is no less deleterious than if it had been planned to do harm. Think about the meetings you attend in which people are afraid to speak up, to confront, to oppose, and even to question. Or the executive who is so intimidating that people merely nod their heads in rote agreement. Or the policy that is so old it has become a company artifact that no one dares challenge.

A case in point: Hewlett-Packard has boasted of a philosophy called The HP Way which has been distilled down from the days of Hewlett and Packard themselves (who really did found the company in a garage and based their work on providing high quality, reliable equipment at a fair price). This belief system is so strong that all new employees receive a book on the topic.

But I found The HP Way to be distorted out of all context from its original meaning. In the late nineties and moving into the twenty-first century, HP had developed an almost evangelically consensus culture. This meant that there was never open disagreement

Case Study

Lest you believe that misguided beliefs and weak premises aren't major problems, consider this.

I was working with one of the largest and most successful organizations in the world, long considered by the business press to be an exemplar of integrity and ethical conduct, while also providing shareholders with industry-leading returns. It was high on the most admired list.

Yet I found in conducting focus groups on diversity, that a sizeable number of middle managers—perhaps as many as 25 percent—absolutely believed that Asians were not fit to hold supervisory positions because they were not able to confront problems directly "due to their culture and heritage." These managers felt they were doing the company and Asian employees a genuine service by steering these individuals into sole contributor jobs in R&D, human resources, finance, and elsewhere.

And, in fact, the number of Asian managers in the organization was inordinately low compared to the number of Asian employees.

If well-run, well-respected, and well-meaning organizations can harbor and support people making this kind of ghastly misjudgment based on their interpretation of the facts, then what's going on every day in most other organizations?

I'll tell you what goes on: A lot of bad decisions based on very bad information and misguided beliefs. It's our job to blow the whistle on this stuff.

If you don't feel you can oppose weak thinking, bad judgment, and faulty reasoning without adverse consequences to your career, then you'd better ask yourself another question: Is this the environment that I consciously choose to support, forge a career in, and seek respect?

at meetings, lack of consensus (sometimes approaching a need for near-unanimity) could derail an otherwise highly attractive initiative, and velocity was seriously slowed by the friction of trying to please all diverse constituencies.

I doubt that's what Hewlett and Packard ever intended, it's clearly not how they built the business when they were running it, and it flies in the face of everything we know about organizational dynamics and innovation. Any dramatic change effort is guaranteed to threaten *someone*, and you can't please all the people all the time (and should never even try to do so). The only thing that rapid consensus readily demonstrates is an unexciting and undemanding proposal.

I think the world of HP, and it's filled with highly intelligent, creative, and articulate people (and it's one of the most gender-blind, color-blind, origin-blind, disability-blind organizations I've ever seen in 30 years of consulting). Yet even in this great company, a very primal belief system can screw up the works. As one of my HP clients told me in stark but colorful terms, "We like to bring you in because you're not afraid to put the dead rat on the table and say, 'We have a dead rat here that you refuse to talk about, so let's consider what to do about it.' "

We talk about "elephants in the room." I like the dead rat analogy even better. This thing is unsightly, it stinks, and we can't keep pretending we don't see it or smell it. What should we do about it?

Finally, some techniques to confront and resolve disagreements about basic premises:

✔ Never make it personal. "You know, I've heard from a lot of people that we're below the industry averages in turnover, despite losing so many good people last year. Do you know what the source is for those statistics?"

✔ Cite evidence, not opposing opinion. "I'm aware of the general belief that our customers prefer an automated response system, so I was wondering what you make of the fact that 9 of 10 customers I talked to just last week told me that our system was cumbersome and they wished they could see a representative more often"

✔ The bigger they are, the harder they listen. Don't hold back because of position. "I'm sensitive to the fact that this memo will go out over your signature as general manager of the division, and I'm wondering if you'll allow me to investigate some of the bases for the conclusions before you make it official"

✔ If at first you don't succeed . . . "I know we discussed this just last week, but since then I've learned that we actually have statistics on total compensation compared to field productivity, and the two track as correlations beyond any statistical error. Shouldn't we revisit our belief about depressed productivity?"

When considering the value proposition, bear in mind that every client deserves a good deal. I'm continually asked by consultants, "How do I prove there's a good deal here?" I'm reluctant to rely on formulas, but here's one that will stand you in good stead, and avoid the dreadful "four levels" nonsense that permeates the training and HR ranks.

Simply take the tangible outcomes (e.g., increased sales or reduced turnover) and multiply by the expected duration of that benefit; then take the intangible outcomes (e.g., reduced stress, better public image) and multiply by the emotional impact (e.g., positive feeling about work, less customer resistance to change); and finally take the peripheral benefits (e.g., awards for good place to work, complimentary magazine articles) and variables positively affected (e.g., government regulatory time reduced, more job candidates seek you out); then divide by the fixed investment.

If you can't provide a whopping ROI in this manner, then there is something wrong with the buyer, with you, or with the project.

The time to confront is early in the consulting process when you're formulating the proposal, and before the actual intervention has begun. Because if faulty premises undermine the project, it's not going

$$\frac{\text{tangible outcomes} \quad \times \text{expected duration of outcomes}}{\text{fixed investment required}}$$

$$+ \text{ intangible outcomes} \times \text{emotional impact of intangibles}$$

$$+ \text{ peripheral benefits}$$

$$+ \text{ variables positively effected}$$

$$= \text{Client's Good Deal}$$

FIGURE 6.5 The client's Good Deal

to be the buyer who is to blame for the weak foundation. It will be you for having operated without questioning it.

SUGGESTED READING

Innovation and Entrepreneurship, by Peter Drucker (Harper & Row, 1984). Of course, virtually any book by Peter Drucker is well worth the time. This one focuses on how to create change and innovation within organizations, no matter how hidebound or conservative they may have become.

PART THREE

THE INTERVENTION

The Pros and Cons of Living There

How to Maximize Strengths and Minimize Weaknesses

THE BEAUTY OF INSTITUTIONAL MEMORY

To my mind, the core advantage of internal consultants and change agents is that they live on the premises and can tap into institutional memory. In fact, one of my major requests over the past few years is to help clients retain their "institutional DNA" amidst voluntary and involuntary change and constant movement of people.

Institutional memory is not merely about the old days. It should encompass these aspects of organizational life:

✔ The founding or origins of the business, especially as they influence current behaviors. The best examples, perhaps, would be The HP Way and the value systems of Hewlett and Packard, who began the great company in their garage; or the founding of FedEx by Fred Smith, who received a grade of C for a hub-and-spoke delivery proposal in a college class, and who reputedly met an early payroll by winning a key poker game late one night.

✔ Memorable employee exploits and accomplishments. Most sales organizations can tell you about the huge sale that an ace salesperson pulled off while flying cross-country. My favorite FedEx story is that of the employee who didn't have a key to open a deposit box, so he pried the entire thing up, loaded it into his truck, and a bevy of workers pounced on it with crowbars and sledges until it could be successfully loaded onto the

---

Case Study

Prudential Insurance has gone through hard times in the past decade, weathering securities scandals and questionable practices. But when I joined them in 1968 fresh out of college, the place was, indeed, a rock of conservative, secure trust for millions of policyholders. And that trust was taken quite seriously.

As a management intern, I had to read a book, commissioned by Prudential, which told of how John Thurber founded the company and used a huge rock structure in Secaucus, New Jersey (the Pru is headquartered in nearby Newark) that reminded him of the Rock of Gibraltar as his symbol of strength. (Hence, "a piece of the rock" in its advertising over the years.)

There was a Prudential museum complete with curator, which housed everything from early employee dress to the first punch card machines and various insurance advances over the decades. We were steeped in the history and values of the company, which helped enormously to understand what business we were in and why.[1]

---

[1]Some of the institutional culture was so strong that it outlasted current tastes and mores, such as the Miss Prudential contest, which featured secretaries and even supervisors in swimsuits parading on a runway with managers as judges. It was standing room only and, even at the time, conveyed a feeling of being in an alternative universe. I never did get to be a judge.

Memphis-bound flight. Note that these stories may be apocryphal—that doesn't really matter in terms of the culture they convey and perpetuate.

✔ Lessons learned from victories and defeats. The latter are as important as the former. The key client who lost because of lack of responsiveness generally sets the tone for future responsiveness. A technological breakthrough that never was operationalized casts a certain pall over technology.

> Institutional memory is like a supertanker, not a speedboat. It can change course, but requires a lot of room and advance preparation. That's why the people already on the ship are best to plot the change, not someone dropped by a helicopter who doesn't even understand all the controls.

✔ Those belief systems that govern behavior, aka "culture." Culture is fungible, but it must be actively managed by reinforcing the desired beliefs and discouraging the nondesired beliefs. IBM took forever to change until the conservative Big Blue mentality and sacrosanct position of the field force was effectively challenged. But it took a new CEO to do it. Corporate culture is not an immutable force, but rather a manageable influence. But you have to work in it and with it every day to create effective and long-lived change. Disney has done this beautifully, maintaining the allure and chasteness of the theme parks while also adapting to the times (and to the different countries in which it operates). The U.S. Postal Service has never mastered the ability to change its own culture—as I write this, there are hundreds of millions of dollars in employee grievances awaiting resolution, and the resolution process alone will cost tens of millions, no matter which side is right.

✔ The way in which people advance, and who the good guys and bad guys are. If people advance through meeting goals no matter what the human cost, that says one thing, while advancement through meeting goals *and* proper treatment of employees and customers means another. Competitors who have stolen ideas and employees are usually well-known, as are those to whom one can always go for help—the "go to" people. This is so strong in some organizations that you find near cultlike atmospheres, such as the enmity between Kamatsu and Caterpillar, Continental and United Airlines at mutual hubs such as Denver, and GM and Ford. In strong product-driven companies, such as Procter & Gamble, it can also be found between product groups or among silos. Turf wars are institutional memory phenomena, no less than the Hatfields and McCoys.

Internal people have the distinct advantage in any intervention of understanding corporate memory and using those elements to support the intended result and not oppose it (or at least to neutralize the potential obstacles and barriers). External people are constantly stepping on land mines in these areas, suddenly finding that the financial department is not cooperating at all in a cost-cutting initiative, despite the last client's CFO's willingness to help, and all indications that there would be no problem with this client. But external people might not have found out that the CFO won't back anything supported by the COO, whose job she once coveted.

> Interventions are dynamic and unstable by nature. They can't be scripted or choreographed, which is why you find no detailed models in this book. Your job as change agent is to blend the various corporate beliefs, traditions, history, and values into a supporting force. That's not easy, but it's easier for an insider.

The few cons in this area for you, however, are severe. If you are identified with a cultural artifact or historical disaster, your credibility (or lack thereof) will undermine attempts to forge new alliances and meld existing beliefs. That's why the identity of your department and the identity of your personal talents are and should be two different things. If your department has a sterling reputation, then you are in a wonderful position to build on it, but that is not generally the way in which human resources, training, internal consulting, and similar functions are viewed, unfortunately (though often deservedly).

I like to think of myself as a corporate therapist, and here's an example loosely adapted from the field of psychology, which should help your own perspective of how you can readily utilize your unique cultural position (see Figure 7.1).

In Figure 7.1, the intent is to demonstrate that you can't resolve a generalized anxiety (e.g., "morale should be better"). You must break it

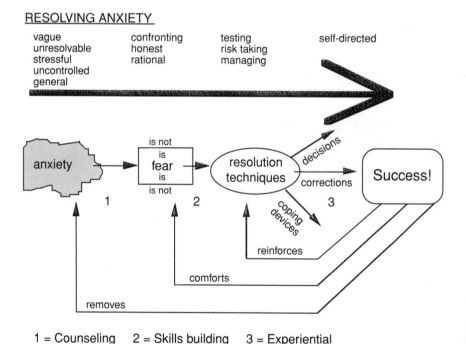

RESOLVING ANXIETY

1 = Counseling   2 = Skills building   3 = Experiential

FIGURE 7.1 Analyzing where to enter a situation

into tangible components (e.g., "our turnover is too high" or "employee grievances are escalating").[2]

It's vital to appreciate the company history, but not to be associated with silos, turf, sides, or blind initiatives. (This is where an executive says, "Let's train the administrative staff in that new Open Mind accountability approach," without any notion of objectives for doing so, measurement of progress, ownership of the audience, and so on, yet everyone scurries to find a vendor.) Only then can resolution techniques be introduced (including learning to cope with the unresolvable) and success ensue. The key for you as a consultant/therapist is to understand *where you are entering the process*, and to obtain the buyer's agreement about the starting point. There is a huge difference between beginning at the experiential aspect versus the counseling aspect, for example. I would contend that internal consultants have a huge advantage when projects and challenges are viewed in this context.

Overall, the pros are far, far more in favor of the internal change agent, and the cons eminently manageable. In fact, on the face of it, you'd have to wonder why an organization would ever seek help on the outside if internal resources are extant. But they do so all the time, and that's often because the internal people can't get out from under all that organizational weight.

LOOKING OUTSIDE THE
ORGANIZATIONAL FOOTPRINT

Having stipulated the advantages of being a part of institutional memory, let's also make clear that the critical value that internal people can create is combining that intimacy with the willingness and means to look outside the past and the culture. I call this an escape from the organizational "footprint."

I loved the footprint phrase, which I first heard in this context when I was having computer hardware installed. The footprint became the amount of space taken up, and soon there were fax foot-

---

[2]I'm not sure who, but some wag observed that therapy is the act of taking a general unhappiness and turning it into stark, raving fear.

prints, copier footprints, phone systems footprints, and so on. The goal became how best to use the interstitial space—the free room not under a footprint.

The same applies to synthesizing organizational change. While there is a distinct advantage in being a part of the culture and breathing the climate every day, the true uniqueness is in the ability to effectively combine that knowledge with the state-of-the-art. What is happening elsewhere in terms of:

✔ Best practices.

✔ Industry standards.

✔ Literature and research.

✔ Professional and trade associations.

✔ Networking with peers.

✔ The competition.

✔ Customers and vendors.

✔ Creativity and innovation.

It seems to me that there are two equally noxious extremes to avoid. The first is the incestuous, inward-staring philosophy that rationalizes "We've always done it this way" and epitomizes rejection through "Not invented here." But the second is the low self-esteem, highly cynical "The grass is always greener" and "If you have such a good idea, why haven't we already done it?" Looking *solely* to the inside or *solely* to the outside is a purblind course.

The finest internal change agents I've ever observed had the discipline, ability, and maturity to select the best from internal history and culture, and best from external practices and resources, and synthesize the two into highly successful, powerful change agents. For example, during a 12-year tenure as a consultant to Merck, from 1987 to 1999, during a period of tremendous profit growth and other achievements,[3]

---

[3]For example, Merck unseated IBM during this period as America's Most Admired Company in *Fortune* magazine's annual poll, and went on to win that honor an unprecedented five consecutive years.

I worked on more than 30 projects, but always in conjunction and partnership with Merck's own human resources, training, and coaching professionals. For most of that period the senior vice president of human resources, Steve Darien, and one of his directors, Art Strohmer, consistently sought out and hired excellent external resources to partner with internal people on major projects.

> The combination of people who know the culture, politics, and environment, and people who know of best practices elsewhere and aren't intimidated by culture, politics, and environment, represent a powerful alliance.

In the 1990s I had the privilege of working consistently with Marilyn Martiny, an internal change agent at Hewlett-Packard, who worked with scores of outside people, often forming virtual consulting teams of internal and external resources that regularly outbid major external consulting firms for projects. When I asked what the appeal was to her and to the company of partnering with so many of us—and especially solo practitioners and small firms, not just the giants—she gave me a classic response: "We want to make sure," she explained, "that we don't start breathing our own exhaust."

I've used that quote countless times since.

Most organizational managers—particularly those with line responsibilities—will have their noses pressed too tightly against the glass of their own goals, customer segments, and competitive concerns to take much time considering factors other than those they are accustomed to. The role of the internal consultant has to be to pry them away from the glass with appealing examples and rationale from outside that organizational footprint.

I'm not suggesting that the only way to create effective internal change is to bring in outside resources. As that outside resource, I don't even believe that, and I've too often been brought in unnecessarily. I am suggesting that internal people, even with the luxury of organizational intimacy, best fulfill their own roles when they reach out to con-

Case Study

I was asked to work with the British Standards Institute[4] as the European Community moved closer to formalization. The client was interested in improving the innovative culture and becoming more proactive and aggressive. It was feared that their monopolistic position in British business would be threatened by Continental competitors once trade barriers were removed.

Over the course of a week, top management teams diligently prepared plans and specific examples of how to gain a market edge across Europe. The best of the best were chosen for a special presentation on the final morning for the managing director (MD), who made the trip down from the London headquarters to our site.

After four of the six presentations without a word from the MD, he finally stood up and said, "For goodness sake, if these were really such good ideas we would have done them ages ago. We're going to have to look to the competition if we're to find really original approaches." And with that, he left.

This was the most extreme case of "grass is greener" that I've ever encountered, and it effectively ended the project, despite the work of the internal change people, senior management, and me. Sometimes there simply is no substitute to strong leadership, and there is no antidote for stupid leadership, internally or externally.

sider and incorporate practices and approaches from outside the organization. That might be nothing more than research and reviews of literature, but it may sometimes extend to actual collaboration with external consultants. My point is that there is a range of potential symbiotic combinations, and that range should at least be reviewed.

---

[4]This organization is charged with setting and monitoring standards for everything from the composition of concrete to the heat levels of toasters.

Once an intervention has begun, and the need emerges for an external person, internal credibility is generally shot. The wound may not be fatal, but it is damaging. However, if that determination is made in the formulation stages, and the original methodology includes the use of outsiders, then their inclusion is planned and smart, not a reaction of desperation. (And not a firefighter arriving to save the burning building.)

> Generally, the more complex the emotional, political, and cultural issues, the *more* an outsider is required. The ability to utilize someone whose retirement plan, benefits, bonus, and career track does *not* depend on the organization is of major assistance. The key is to hire, manage, and control those resources as an intelligent aspect of your project, and not to have them foisted upon you in an attempt to save your project.

In the preponderance of cases, if I'm initially contacted by senior or line management, I know that internal resources:

✔ Aren't available, or
✔ Are not trusted, or
✔ Have already failed, or
✔ Have refused the assignment (unlikely).

If, however, I'm initially contacted by internal change agents, then I know that these people:

✔ Are confident, and
✔ Are seeking the best combinations of resources, and
✔ Have credibility with management, and
✔ Their recommendations will be seriously considered.

Even if the ultimate hiring is by the actual buyer (internal consultants and human resource peoples are seldom buyers—they don't have the budgets or the final decision, though they may be very critical recommenders to the buyer), in the latter case the endorsement by the internal people is tantamount to being hired.

So the combination of being historically and culturally educated and sensitive, and of being willing and able to access a range of outside assistance (from research and best practices through interactive help) make the internal change agent a unique and potentially irreplaceable contributor. Neither position alone is adequate. At one extreme is the insistence on doing everything internally (a human resources director at Southwest Airlines claimed once in a speech that consultants simply don't know what she and her colleagues know, and that's about as blind a view as I've ever heard). At the other extreme is the blind purchase of external help without even sufficient need having been determined (which is why training vendors sells hundreds of thousands of dollars of materials to trainers who believe that simply putting people in classrooms helps performance, without regard to objectives, measures, or actual discernible change).

Actually, it's not a very fine line to walk. It's rather broad if you stay sober and walk straight, without becoming intoxicated by fads or egos and straying too far from the center.

FORCE FIELD ANALYSES

In every consulting project of any impact, there are forces that encourage and discourage success. We know this. The trouble is, we too often ignore this.

> Whenever it seems like a project is a lock and that success is assured, that's precisely the time to crawl under a table and protect yourself. Because it's even money that the roof is about to fall down.

Consulting isn't a crap shoot, where we've placed money on the pass line and hope we don't throw a 12. Consulting is art and science, probably more the former than the latter in most cases, and requires some careful planning and choreography in an attempt to maximize our chances of success.

External consultants are at still another disadvantage here. They don't know all the factors mitigating for and against; they don't have time to investigate them; they have to rely on others' (biased) views of support; and they often learn of opposition too late to prevent it and of support too late to exploit it. Conversely, internal people have the luxury of usually being able to carefully evaluate the forces aligned pro and con, and can do some early work to further influence the opposition and rally the supporters. There's just no substitute for being there.

Yet this advance preparation often doesn't occur. Internal people walk into a project voluntarily wearing the same blinders that external people are desperately and frantically trying to shed. That sure does level the playing field, although I can't imagine why external consultants should be blessed with such largesse.

The forces in most organizations that will influence organizational change projects one way or the other usually include:[5]

✔ Direct reports of the buyer.

✔ Informal leaders (e.g., top salespeople, union officers, etc.).

✔ Customers.

✔ Vendors.

✔ Other, affected departments.

✔ Implementers themselves (e.g., front line supervisors).

✔ Prevailing culture.

✔ Precedent for such change.

✔ Physical environment and facilities.

✔ Equipment: amount, quantity, and capability.

---

[5]This assumes that the buyer is personally a supportive force. In some rare occasions, this may not be the case, for example, "backing" something popular but not personally involved.

✔ Time available to prepare, implement, and fine-tune.

✔ Your personal credibility and power to influence.

✔ Perceived need for the change.

✔ Perception of sacrifice for the change.

✔ Impact on people (e.g., transfers, layoffs, retraining, etc.).

✔ Competing changes and priorities.

✔ Imponderables.

"Imponderables" is my catchall for things like morale, momentum, intuition, and so on. A great many athletic competitions are decided not on superior physical ability or conditioning, but on psychology, performance under pressure, and so forth. This is not a minor factor, so I've made provision for it.

Perhaps you already diligently examine all of these as well as other factors, assess whether they promote or resist your project, and take commensurate action. If so, proceed to the next section. But I doubt that many of you are going to make that leap.

Consultants generally ignore the force field analysis that is necessitated by these factors, and consequently stroll into a project with no more preparation than warming up the dice with encouraging words. While external consultants have the half-excuse of not being aware of the orientation of these factors, *they are nevertheless aware that the factors exist and need to be plumbed.* Internal consultants have no excuse for ignoring these key determinants (other than sloth).

If you don't know who's with you and who's against you, how do you know whom to welcome and whom to fear, or when to laugh and when to smile? When you don't know where the land mines are, *every path must be a cautious one.* That leads to an awfully slow and arduous journey.

Let's take a sample instance to experiment with our force field analysis. You have been approached with a project to change the company call center (your first major project in the six months you've been with the organization) so that it makes outgoing sales calls as well as receiving orders and requests for technical support. Such aggressive telemarketing is unprecedented in the firm, and will surely overwhelm both the skills and numbers of the current three dozen full- and part-time telephone representatives. The primary products sold are basic office supplies: toner, paper, staples, envelopes, and so on.

The initiative was requested by the vice president of sales to offset the high acquisition costs of the force field by making calls to high-potential buyers—usually medium-sized firms' office managers—who may not require face-to-face meetings because they know their needs well and have authority to spend at least $500 per purchase. The call center manager, who reports to the vice president of operations (who gave her blessing to the project but is not funding it) is clearly against the change, knowing that she, personally, has no sales background and no desire for selling.

Ironically, there was no force field (only catalog sales) up to five years ago, and the new force field at the time, fiercely resisted, proved to be the key to improving revenues by more than 50 percent. The remainder of the organization—manufacturing, finance, operations—is on a profit sharing plan, so anything to increase sales and profits is generally supported.

The sales force is very concerned about lost commissions to phone sales. And the sales vice president is funding the changes by not hiring several salespeople for whom he has approved and budgeted slots, demanding that the field force "do more with less." You've been told that it would be important to make the shift in about 90 days, prior to the traditionally heavy fall season.

Using these factors, rate each one either + for a positive force, – for a negative force, 0 for neutral, or ? for unknown. Here's the list again:

Factor	*Rating*
✔ Direct reports of the buyer.	_____
✔ Informal leaders.	_____
✔ Customers.	_____

✔ Vendors. _____

✔ Other, affected departments. _____

✔ Implementers themselves. _____

✔ Prevailing culture. _____

✔ Precedent for such change. _____

✔ Physical environment and facilities. _____

✔ Equipment: amount, quantity, and capability. _____

✔ Time available to prepare, implement, fine-tune. _____

✔ Your personal credibility and power to influence. _____

✔ Perceived need for the change. _____

✔ Perception of sacrifice for the change. _____

✔ Impact on people. _____

✔ Competing changes and priorities. _____

✔ Imponderables. _____

Even some rigorous opposition tends to fall into line when early successes show that an initiative is actually going to improve everyone's lot to the extent that minor inconvenience and short-term unhappiness can be justified. That is one of the imponderables to consider.

I'm not asking whether you would take the project or not, but how much advance work you'd have to do to change the prevailing forces more in your favor. Here's my evaluation.

Factor

✔ Direct reports of the buyer. – This is a negative because the direct reports are the people running the field force and aren't going to be enamored by dealing with the ensuing complaints and probably perceived loss for their own incentive income.

✔ Informal leaders.   – It would seem to me that the call center's current leadership is not going to support a move that might change their stature.

✔ Customers.   + It's easy to order by phone, and too time-consuming to spend time in the office with vendors. In addition, an unwanted sales phone call can be easily ignored or quickly rebuffed.

✔ Vendors.   + They shouldn't care one way or the other, although increased sales will improve their business, so the edge goes to the positive here.

✔ Other, affected departments.   0 Except for sales, no one should care one way or the other.

✔ Implementers themselves.   – The call center will no doubt have some people who are enthusiastic about new opportunities, but most will no doubt resist and be fearful of their future.

✔ Prevailing culture.   + Outside of sales and the call center, this will probably be embraced.

✔ Precedent for such change.   + The field force itself began with massive change, and this seems less complex.

✔ Physical environment and facilities.   + These apparently exist, though they might need modest expansion.

✔ Equipment: amount, quantity, and capability.   + These, too, seem to be in place and might only require expansion.

✔ Time available to prepare, implement, fine-tune.   – Given the probable need for changes in skills and new additions, 90 days seems like far too little time.

✔ Your personal credibility and power to influence.   0 I'm calling this a neutral, on the assumption that you haven't insulted anyone or made a fool of yourself in the prior six months. But you have no track record, either.

✔ Perceived need for the change.   ? Tough call. The buyer certainly sees it, as do probably his peers, but the call center doesn't and the field force probably doesn't, so I've rated it a toss-up until I can find out (or influence it).

✔ Perception of sacrifice for the change. – There will be substantial sacrifice in at least two areas, call center and sales.

✔ Impact on people. – This is negative, at least for the short-term.

✔ Competing changes and priorities. + There were no competing projects or priorities mentioned, so the focus can be exclusive.

✔ Imponderables. + I'm estimating that if we can achieve some small victories early (e.g., initial sales by phone, some leads for larger business sent to the sales force, some customer satisfaction surveys) things may just fall into place quickly.

> The point of force field analysis is to understand what your early battle plan should be. There are few fights that can't be won at all, and equally few that require no effort. If you don't know the pros and cons, then you don't know your assets and liabilities.

My final tally: 6 negatives, 8 positives, 2 neutrals, and 1 question mark. How did you evaluate this? It's not the answer that counts (remember that this is more art than science) but your rationale based on the facts presented.[6] In traditional force field representation, my assessment would look something like Figure 7.2.

Consequently, your goal is to eliminate, reduce, or circumvent the restraining factors while exploiting the promoting factors. That may mean co-opting a few of the informal leaders and direct reports, changing the perception of sacrifice with solid job offers in other areas for those who want to transfer, moving fast to take advantage of limited time while no conflicting priorities exist, and so on.

---

[6] In all candor, I thought I had written a far more negative scenario, but in actually evaluating it, I realized that it was more positive than I had envisioned. You never know until you use some discipline.

Restraining Factors

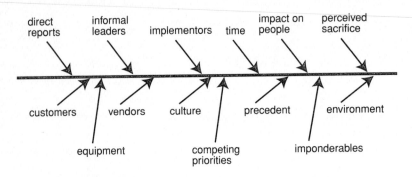

Promoting Factors

FIGURE 7.2   Force field analysis of case study

Final comment: If you're not doing a methodical and disciplined force field analysis prior to your actual intervention, you've discarded most of your advantage as an internal practitioner and, worse, cheated your client out of the maximum measures to ensure success before you begin. You're at the craps table, not the drafting table.

COMBATING PEOPLE LIKE ME

Here's a section I always wanted to write. What if I were an internal consultant (I was, in the late 1960s, at Prudential) and was in competition with external consultants for prime pieces of business?[7] How would I act and what would I do? How do I prevent Alan from taking my rightful business?

Internal people should be involved in *every* project. That's right,

---

[7]In fact, most competition an external consultant faces is not from other external resources, but from internal resources.

If a major initiative is under way without the involvement of the recognized internal change agents, then there is no reason to be in your position at all. Major sales efforts don't exist without the key sales leaders, and significant R&D projects are supervised by the proper R&D management. Why should consulting be any different?

every one. There are two basic dimensions in which you can and should be involved.

1. Solely Internal. This comprises business that is either best handled internally or can be handled equally well internally or externally (so why go outside at all?).

   The best way to keep the likes of me from this project is to maximize a combination of the following factors:

   ✔ Maintain close relationships with key department and functional leaders (your potential buyers).

   ✔ Publish internally, in the house organ, the company magazine, on the corporate web site.

   ✔ Develop a strong reference and referral list within your own company.

   ✔ Volunteer ideas, resources, and value in general to potential buyers—be proactive, not solely reactive.

   ✔ Demonstrate a cost effectiveness for internal focus.[8] Despite an external consultant's fixed fee and lack of fringes, show that the internal work—including salary allocation and any charge-backs—will be far more economical in

---

[8]I'm very accomplished at demonstrating that external resources are actually more cost effective, so this isn't as easy as it may sound.

terms of follow-up, refinements, round-the-clock attention, and so on.

✔ Determine the external resource's vulnerabilities. Many external consultants, for example, continue to foolishly bill by the hour or day, so you can make a case for avoiding a meter running and the inherent conflict of building hours in order to build fees. Or make a case for the costs involved while the consultant is learning your business, or that the principal will disappear once the project is signed, leaving junior people with you.

✔ Offer a test or pilot—a free, dry run to show how you'd handle it. Gain some easy, early victories and you should be home free.

2. Combination internal and external. There are absolutely valid occasions when external resources are required. For example:

✔ Best practices and first-hand knowledge of them are desired.

✔ A nonpolitical, nonpartisan, nonemployee's objectivity is sought.

✔ A specialist or acclaimed authority is desired.

✔ A peer reference to the buyer has promoted the external resource as invaluable and perfect for the needs.

✔ The buyer knows someone from a former life whom he or she implicitly trusts.

But no matter how strong these reasons, they *don't preclude an internal resource*, but simply specify external involvement. You can't cede the field and admit some kind of silly defeat or, worse, try to undermine the external effort to prove the decision was wrong.[9] (Undermining the project

---

[9]Internal sabotage, contrary to the perpetrators' beliefs, is as obvious as a ham sandwich, and any external consultant worth his Palm Pilot will readily report resistance to the buyer, because it's really the only professional thing to do with it.

> I had arrived at a Fortune 50 company to begin a project, and found a deputation of human resources people who requested a meeting. Anxiously, I sat down and, to my shock, listened to them proclaim, "We want you to know how glad we are you're here. You'll tell them the same thing we've been saying for two years, but because of your fee, now they'll listen!" I walked out relieved but also depressed by their desperation.

will make you look petty if it fails and like an ass if it succeeds despite you.)

The key that most internal resources have not mastered is how to *effectively partner* with external consultants, no matter how they enter the organization. Here's how you do it, pure and simple, seven steps to take your rightful place in the project's progress:

1. Introduce yourself. If you haven't been introduced or deliberately involved, take this on yourself. External consultants will not, generally, take pains to meet the internal people who may have been snubbed.

2. Provide value. Explain the background, environment, culture, and circumstances leading to this particular project. Offer assistance with anything the external consultant might not understand. (External people often feel forced to make some leaps of faith and assumptions rather than ask questions that may make them seem uninformed. This offer will usually be warmly received.)

3. Ask for some participation. Don't tap-dance around the issue. Demonstrate that you can be of help and that there is a lot more value still to be had. If necessary, specify some dirty jobs or unique areas where you can alleviate some of the burden.

4. Make your involvement clear to the buyer. Ask the consultant to mention your involvement to ensure full disclosure. Try to become involved in meetings, reports, briefings, and other interactions. Don't be content with backstage participation. Play a strong and visible supporting role.

5. Meet frequently (or at least communicate frequently) with the consultant. Force the partnership to evolve. For example, you should never allow an on-site visit to take place without at least a quick meeting or lunch with the consultant. If he or she doesn't visit frequently (I generally don't), then reach out at least once a week by phone and/or e-mail.

6. Volunteer to be a part of the follow-up and continued reinforcement. This is one of the great weaknesses of external consulting—you ultimately must pack up and go home. Your ongoing participation will serve to make everyone look good.

7. If possible, arrange for transfer of the long-term measurement, updates, and tweaking completely to you. Make the transfer back to internal focus complete.

If you can't effectively partner with external resources, then you may not be cut out for the consulting role. External resources must partner with internal people every single time. Why should you be exempt from this requirement?

Are these steps always possible? I don't know, but I do know that they are *seldom even attempted*. Don't throw up your hands and lament your fate when someone like me walks in the door. Understand that I just may be your brightest opportunity.

SUGGESTED READING

Presentation Jazz: How to Make Your Sales Presentations Sing by Anne Miller (amacom, 1998). These are useful tips for anyone trying to influence management to invest in something, so why shouldn't they apply to internal people, as well?

Chapter 8

The Politics of Terror

How to Reconcile Tough Issues without Being Drawn and Quartered

FACTUAL VERSUS EMOTIONAL CONFRONTATION

Consulting projects often get ugly. By definition we are roiling the pot: creating change, fixing problems, improving performance, altering habits, removing sinecures, reallocating resources. Somewhere, somehow, someone is going to be upset.

The worst responses to these inherent conflicts and perceived threats is to attempt to create consensus (I hope even the most blissfully optimistic realize that unanimity is not an option). Organizations have clearly defined turf boundaries as well as less clearly demarcated borders of interest and defense. The sales department might be a clear citadel, but within the fortress there are likely to be separate interests by product, geography, tenure, client type, and other criteria.

The best consultants do not go out of their way to alienate people and make enemies, but they also don't sacrifice principles, value, or ethics when facing entrenched and threatening resistance, either.[1] *The*

---

[1]If you find you're constantly compromising and retreating, you may want to refer to the final chapter's final section, When It's Time to Go.

*single greatest advantage of external consultants is that they are in a posi-
tion to resist pressure and are more impervious to threat.*

There's no question that an irate, powerful manager can make
your life miserable. But that's life. Salespeople face the challenge of
battling prospect and customer objections in order to bring home the
sale, make plan, and earn bonus. Managers must fight for their projects with superiors to gain budget, resources, and support. Organizational life is about the healthy reconciliation of competing interests
every single day.

Why should internal consulting be any different, any safer, or any
more comfortable?

> With the inherent advantage of living in the organization, if
> an internal consultant can overcome the fear—real and imag-
> ined—of strong opposition to his or her initiatives, that con-
> sultant will always be a more valuable resource than an
> external consultant. Period.

The best technique for dealing with internal, direct observation is
to discipline yourself to deal with facts, evidence, and observed behavior, and never emotion, supposition, or judgmental biases.

Here, then, are three important guidelines for constructive confrontation (sort of like compassionate conservatism, I guess):

1. *Choose your fights based on project needs.* Every project has
   certain core needs that, if violated, will result in failure. Establish these in advance with your buyer. For example, as
   part of an improved rate of R&D commercialization, it may
   be imperative that sales and R&D form closer links to build
   consumer demands into new products during the design
   phase. But it may not be vital that R&D people speak directly
   to the current customers. That means that you can pull back
   on a suggestion for that direct contact if sales strenuously ob-
   jects, but you can't retreat from creating a procedure whereby

---

Case Study

I'm observing a meeting run by an internal facilitator, who has told me that the finance department is "out to get him," because the project is examining, among other things, delayed financial reporting. There are six people assembled as the meeting gets under way, but the financial representative is not present.

About 10 minutes later, the financial woman arrives and takes her seat. The facilitator tells her, "This is the third meeting in a row you've been late, and I'm wondering if you really want to be on this team. You don't seem to show your colleagues much respect, and I interpret this as deliberate rudeness toward me."

"I'm sorry you see it that way," she coolly responds, "since you never mentioned it to me before. I thought you knew that I'm on flex time and don't start until an hour later, but I come in early just for your meeting. I have to drop my child at day care, which normally isn't a problem, but when there's traffic it makes me about 10 minutes late. You never asked if this was a convenient time for any of us, and I didn't want to ruin your schedule."

After that bit of heavy-handedness, I wouldn't blame her if she were out to get him.

---

sales obtains key customer information on a methodical basis to respond to R&D questions.

Don't get bloody over alternatives when one is as good as another in the long run. Don't defend pet options and private biases. But do stand firm when a key objective of the project, *as agreed with the buyer*, will not be met. This is another example of must/want partition: You can be flexible on the desirables, but you can't negotiate away a mandatory requirement. I've seen countless projects fail when an absolutely vital component was whisked away by a powerful opponent (who nonetheless provided lip-service support).

For example, in the midst of a major emphasis on solution selling at a major high tech company, a highly visible, senior manager in charge of the largest market downsized his solution selling support team. This single move, despite his avowed support for the philosophy, killed the entire project for all practical purposes. He was never called on his move.

During the conceptual agreement phase, establish with your buyer what the three or four nonnegotiable, nonsurrender issues are, and ask for the buyer's unequivocal support if you have to defend those resolutely.

---

2. *Watch your language (and the other person's, too).* Focus on observed behavior and evidence. Back up everything you say with examples. If you use assumptions, identify them, *and specify how you will validate them and when.* Carefully separate fact from opinion, otherwise a bad opinion will also cast doubt on your facts.

Similarly, politely and constructively help others to understand those differences. When someone says, "The field force will not accept any hint of a change to the current compensation plan," reply, "That may be, but how can we find out for sure? We've all been saying that so long that it's become a mantra that may not be true any longer. Two district managers told me personally that they would support certain changes that encouraged new sales over repeat business, for example."

Powerful people have the habit of using their office, their volume, or their reputation as equalizers for fact and opinion. You can't allow that to happen, particularly if a critical portion of the plan is jeopardized.[2] It's often useful to step up to an easel and, like a forensic accountant or a police detective, say, "Let's separate what we absolutely know in this sheet from what we're assuming or guessing on that sheet." Note: The words "we" and "our" and other plural forms help to remove blame from any party and create more of a team-based search for the truth.

For example, I was able to improve the teamwork of 10 direct reports to the general manager of an animal health business when, through interviews and observation, I was able to identify just one of their number who constantly made judgment calls, which he passed off as facts that the others didn't bother challenging. Once they all were required to support opinions with evidence, the internal bickering quickly subsided, as reason replaced emotion.

3. *Focus on the objective, not the alternative.* Most resistance and resultant consultant failure occur where they needn't— over alternatives. In other words, the objective (decrease costs, improve retention, gain market share, build morale, etc.) is always believed to be a worthy goal, even by highly disparate parties. But it's the journey to arrive there that causes bitter reaction.

Focus the resistors on the goal and ask what options are available. *Most conflict of this type arises over pre-established options without the consent of the stakeholders.* If the salespeople don't want third parties contacting their customers, ask them for options that achieve the same ends of independent customer input. If the operations people object to financial reporting on a weekly basis, ask them what other choices there are to guarantee that excessive inventory is being reduced each week.

---

[2]I can make a case that you can't even allow them to do that on minor issues, because it creates a precedent and momentum that carries over to the major issues. "My experience and gut feel were good enough for you yesterday," is a statement that I never want to respond to when opposing that person on another issue the following day. It's a slippery slope.

> Asking other people how they would do it often has the salu-
> tary effects of either generating a far better implementation
> idea, or of convincing them that there is no better way than
> the original one presented. Either outcome is better than re-
> sistance, even if it takes a bit longer.

For example, a team of vice presidents refused to budge when the consultant presented them with a myriad of options to change the incentive compensation system. The force field claimed its objectives were far different from "staff positions," and the nonfield executives believed that their people didn't participate sufficiently in profit sharing. We changed the charge from "select the best option" to "generate the best option or the general manager will simply select one that he feels is best for controlling costs." Within 48 hours we had an excellent compensation plan that was supported by every significant department head.

You can't avoid confrontation on major consulting initiatives, but if you practice these three rules, you'll be able to resolve it or channel it toward constructive outcomes much more readily.

AVOIDING INTERNECINE WARRIORS

Even more nefarious than open confrontation are hidden agendas. At least those openly opposing you are candid and obvious, no matter how truculent and ferocious they may be. It's always best to know the enemy in front of you.

But when the enemy is behind you and doesn't look like the enemy, you have problems.

Internal and external consultants alike are often lured into mercenary status. That is, we're being paid to fight someone else's wars and our particular project is less important than the ultimate victory. We may die in that just cause.

We have become cannon fodder.

Internal warfare is one of the worst aspects of organizational life. In fact, it's one of the reasons I left organizational life. Early in my undergraduate career as a political science major, I learned that war is simply the least subtle form of communication. (And that fact applies to marriages, partnerships, and colleagues, no less than nation–states.) It occurs when all the less physical alternatives have either been unsuccessful, dispensed with, or totally ignored. Warfare is bloody, and people in organizations are wounded, incapacitated, and even killed by it.

Take it from someone who has worked in upward of 1,500 organizations over 30 years, *not all environments are equally political, prone to warfare, or brutal.* Some are clearly worse than others, and they range from the tepidly political to the violently silolike.

> Internal warfare destroys productivity and performance. Consultants must identify it, avoid taking sides even inadvertently, and ultimately defuse it if they are to play any kind of important role in organizational life.

The major performance drawback for such omnipresent combat is illustrated in Figure 8.1.

People have only 100 percent of their talents and energies to dedicate at any one time. "Do more with less" and "give me 110 percent" are meaningless and insulting phrases. We only have 100 percent to give, so the question is: *How much of that talent and energy can be focused externally—on the product, service, relationship, and customer— and how much will be frittered away internally—on combat, politics, turf issues, and jealousies?*

Your job is to focus your own energies outside the circle as well as the energies and talents of your colleagues and stakeholders. That means fundamentally and primarily the avoidance of taking sides.

Ultimately, you may come out on one side or another, as your work demonstrates that one party has more legitimate points than an-

Where Are the Resources Going?

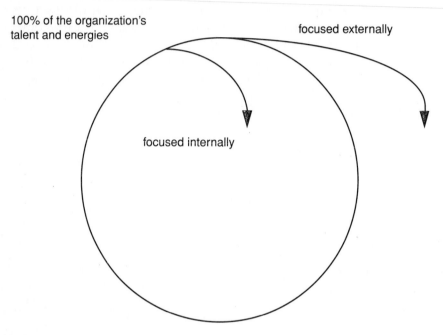

100% of the organization's talent and energies

focused externally

focused internally

FIGURE 8.1 The allocation of resources, internally vs. externally

other. But that's the result of your diagnostic work, and not the starting bias that begins the work.

People at war are often quite powerful and command impressive armaments. Worse, however, they can be subtle and persuasive, and play to your ego, meaning that you are the White Knight leading a worthy cause. Just remember that knights become cannon fodder, too.

Here are four ways to identify, dissect, and enter a consulting proposition that involve warring parties and live to tell about it.

1. *Don't accept right and wrong opening gambits.* Organizational life is not like an off and on switch; it is like a rheostat, changing brightness and hues by subtle advances or retreats. When the buyer says that the objective is to "overcome the foot dragging of operations," or "show sales once and for all that they

can't keep underestimating revenues," stop right there and ask, "What prompted this need?" That will move the conversation to "slow customer order fulfillment," or "overpayments on compensation compared to actual orders." Those are legitimate grounds for investigation.

2. *Seek cause, not blame.* Your job is to find out why something is going wrong or not improving, not to advance an inquisition. Too often projects begin with "If the vice president of strategy were removed, we wouldn't even be talking." Don't accept assignments with a target. Accept assignments only with a clear business outcome. (Firing someone is not a business outcome by any definition.)[3]

> Beware the warrior who is popular and has won all prior battles. That person may only be a despot, with frightened followers, who will inevitably some day meet a more powerful adversary.

3. *Immediately work with all sides.* Do not allow the work to proceed—even for a few days—focused on your benefactor's side only (or any one side). You will become aligned with it by perception. Diligently divide your time among all camps. Perform the same functions—interviewing, observation, focus groups, training, whatever—and make sure you involve the top people in each function. It's far harder to ignore or denigrate someone who is a personal contact than it is an unnamed and unseen consultant or HR type believed to be a subversive working for the opposition. Get involved with everyone, and quickly.

4. *Be fearless in your assessment.* Life is short. Once you have the facts, be clear and objective. You might find mutual fault, or

[3]Not infrequently, this lament is, "We have to circumvent that HR bunch of bureaucrats!"

more parochial culpability. Back up whatever you find with hard evidence and observed behavior, don't use personalities at all, and offer clear and specific suggestions for reconciling the situation. Here's a poor analysis: "The customer service manager and distribution manager hate each other, and don't collaborate on rush orders, hoping the other will look bad to management." Here's a better version: "The general manager should establish a guideline for delivering special client orders and enforce a zero-tolerance policy in terms of deviations from it. The distribution and customer service managers are accountable for meeting that standard jointly, and both are to be evaluated monthly for conformance with it. Actual performance should be measured by the daily special orders summary issued by accounting."

If you find yourself negotiating or assisting in negotiations, try to implement a rational negotiating model. Figure 8.2 is one example.

This is an intelligent approach to resolving conflict be it with

START

Establish nonviolable musts.

Establish a constructive tone but on your turf, or neutral turf.

If possible, have subordinates begin discussions.

When you are involved, listen much more than you talk.

Concede "wants" when necessary, but never "musts."

Always focus on the other side's value, not the price or cost.

Do not concede price without a tangible reduction in value.

Summarize to ensure that all parties understand the same facts.

Put it in writing.

FINISH

FIGURE 8.2 A negotiating sequence

your client, among clients, among stakeholders, or with any other parties. You may have an even better approach, but the key is to have some methodical sequence in place.

Avoid internecine wars. The life you save just could be your own.

PERSUASION THROUGH SELF-INTEREST

There are only three methods I've ever seen employed to create behavior change on the job. This applies to all situations, from influencing buyers to make a decision to gaining the movement necessary from stakeholders to implement an initiative.

The problem is that two of them don't work. (When legendary Ohio State football coach Woody Hayes was asked why his teams always ran and rarely passed the ball, he observed, "When you pass, three things can happen, and two of them are bad. Now why would we want to do that?")

> There is a fundamental difference between compliance and commitment. That difference is in *ownership*, which actually refers to the degree that an individual believes that a change will be personally rewarding.

The basic, fundamental, primal, let's-not-kid-ourselves, keep-it-simple change agents:

1. *Coercion.* In the schoolyard, coercion meant a punch in the head, or assignment as an outcast and pariah. In the workplace, it rarely (though sometimes) means brute force. It usually includes, however:

   ✔ Power to reward: evaluations, assignments, credit, money, and so on.

   ✔ Power to punish: the negative application of the above factors.

✔ Ostracizing from the in crowd.

✔ Direct threats from superiors.

✔ Being saddled with blame or culpability for failure.

Consultants rarely can use coercion to influence buyers and clients, but can often advertently and inadvertently apply such pressure to stakeholders (e.g., "I'll be forced to include your refusal to participate and provide resources in my report to the management team on Friday").

The use of brute force and power can gain movement, but not motivation. Consequently, change based on the application of power is effective only so long as the power is directly applied and there is genuine fear of its use. Once it is learned that the threat is empty,[4] people will quickly revert to preferred behaviors. Moreover, there's always the chance that someone will come along with a larger, countervailing threat, that is, another department head or informal leader who may encourage resignations, transfers, opposing incentives, and so on.

A note here on motivation. Motivation is inherent. That is, I can't motivate you and you can't motivate me, which is why motivational speakers pack the nutritional equivalent of a sugar cookie. A temporary high followed by no lasting positive effects and some possible cavities. The best we can do is establish an environment that is conducive to people becoming motivated. Motivation is self-perpetuating, which is why it provides commitment and not merely compliance.

---

[4]The Prussian Army under Frederick the Great was feared throughout Europe because of its discipline, arms, and leadership, but when it was finally challenged, it turned out that it couldn't fight, and Prussia collapsed. The threat was utilitarian only so long as people were willing to believe it would be applied and would be effective.

2. *Peer Pressure.* The psychologists call this "normative pressure," and it refers to the need to be a part of the "in crowd." Consultants sometimes try to create change through appeals "not to miss the boat" and to "be a part of the team."

   The result on the management level is that buyers and/or key stakeholders may agree to "be on board" but do the least possible work to maintain that "on board" status. They simply want the label but not the accountability. Peer pressure is very ephemeral—it can literally change by the day, sensitive to any number of developments, such as perceived support (or lack of support) from respected leaders, competitive actions, nonrelated events (e.g., a compensation change), and so on.

Case Study

When I had been at Prudential for barely six months, the human resources people came around and asked for a weekly paycheck deduction to support the savings bond campaign. I responded that I was making so little money, and newly married, that I didn't see how I could do it.

They asked me if I wanted to be the sole manager "preventing us from 100 percent participation for this division, which is our general manager's goal." Seeing my management career flash before my eyes, I agreed to the very minimum deduction allowable.

A few months later several of us compared notes, and found that the same threat had been made to all of us, and that participation was actually around the 50 percent level, even among veterans. We all quickly dropped our savings bond deductions, and nothing was ever said.

The only thing worse than no credibility, is having credibility, losing it, and seeking to regain it. Not one of us trusted anything HR ever told us again, no matter how much sense it may have made at the time.

Too many consultants fool themselves by using peer pressure to gain compliance, and then walking away assuming the implementation will proceed *as if there were true commitment.* Peer pressure is virtually worthless as a serious change mechanism. In fact, it is a surrender of leadership to whim and fancy.

3. *Enlightened self-interest.* Think about the qualitatively different responses to these two questions:

✔ Would you like to see my vacation slides?

✔ May I see your vacation slides?

No contest. The second one has me plugging in my projector while the first one has me heading for the exit.

Nothing is as effective in gaining change as appealing to *the other person's* enlightened self-interest.[5] You can more rapidly gain acceptance by a buyer and participation by a stakeholder if they can immediately see in your proposal *what's in it for them.* If that sounds mercenary and selfish, it's not. People make few humanitarian and self-sacrificing decisions. (If you don't believe that, watch people as they exit a religious service commence to battle each other to get out of the parking lot first, often including gestures and phrases you wouldn't see and hear inside of religious service.)[6]

If you want to find the other people's self-interest, *you have to think from the outside-in.* Put yourself in their shoes, use their perspective, look through their eyes. You must achieve what you want through appeals to their needs.

---

[5] I use the qualifier "enlightened" to separate out irrational self-interest, such as gain at others' expense, unrealistic expectations, unethical acts, and so on.
[6] Sure, people support blood drives, charities, and make other sacrifices, but a major component is that they feel good for having done so.

The absolute worst position to be in is to purvey an HR project that is clearly perceived as in your best interest but no one else's. The best position is that you are, with no personal agenda, helping a buyer to meet her sales goals, helping a stakeholder to service his customers more responsively, and assisting the customer to obtain faster service.

The people who are least successful are the demanders—your hotel room has been given away, and you jump and shout and threaten the job of the harried desk clerk. Those who best succeed are the ones who support the other party—"I know this has put you in a terrible position, so let's look at our options together. You must have some VIP suites that you save, and it seems that this is a good example of where one should be used, right?"

Always—every time, unfailingly, *siempre*—view your challenges from the other party's perspective and determine what personal, rational interest will motivate them to commit to supporting your course of action. Ironically, this requires no more expense or work on your part, but *different work*—some homework to understand what dynamics apply.

Ask yourself:

- ✔ What does he need that this project will make possible?
- ✔ Which of her personal and/or professional interests will be served?
- ✔ How will their jobs be made easier?
- ✔ What obstacles to their performance will be removed?
- ✔ How will credit, visibility, and recognition of performance be enhanced?
- ✔ How will relationships be improved?
- ✔ How will stress be alleviated?
- ✔ What new opportunities will be opened?

Finally, understand the close connection between self-interest and true motivation, and that the latter is created *only by the acquisition and successful application of new skills*. Motivation is not some goofy experience in the outdoors, ridiculous self-affirmations ("I AM my own best friend!!!), or nutty book by some temporary television personality. If it were that simple, we'd all be motivated all the time.[7]

Motivation is a function of self-esteem, and actually works as shown in Figure 8.3.

The more you are able to provide tangible, pragmatic, immediately applicable skills and improvements, the more likelihood that the attendant success will create the motivation to want to both reapply those skills continually *and* acquire new skills (particularly from the same source). This is a guarantee of credibility and respect for the consultant.

So make no mistakes: Persuasion and influence are gained through challenging, sound, practical skills acquisition, not by fads

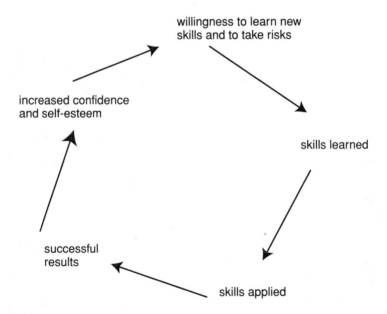

FIGURE 8.3   The self-esteem cycle

[7]Just like all the "make a million" books and opportunities. The only people who make a million are the authors. If the techniques worked, there would be no more need for the books! And do you really want to buy stocks from some guy who has to call you at home at 8 P.M.? Shouldn't he be retired and living on his great investment talent?!

and fakes. If you base your own power on the fad du jour or the guru with the fancy book, you'll find yourself increasingly alienated from your own buyers and stakeholders. But if you see the world through their eyes, and provide the help that accelerates their ability to meet their own personal and professional objectives, you'll be embraced as the most valuable resource around.

It's your choice.

AVOIDING THE SAVIOR COMPLEX

The toughest problem for even high-powered executives whom I coach is terminating people. Contrary to popular opinion, most senior people are not the cold-hearted reptiles depicted in newspaper stories about layoffs, at least not when the decision stops at their desks.

Instead, they are remarkably loath to dismiss even blatantly marginal performers with whom they have any kind of relationship.[8] What they tell me, in so many words, is "Not on my watch."

This is dysfunctional behavior, since it sinks the preponderance of the executive's very expensive time into issues surrounding poor performance, rather than focusing it on superb performance and stellar performers. Organizations don't grow by correcting weaknesses—they grow by building on strengths.

The exact same dynamic holds true for consulting.

Avoiding the savior complex means you have to call 'em as you see 'em, just as a dispassionate athletic official is supposed to do. Not every situation is salvageable, not every person is a candidate for rehabilitation. Often, transgressors must be removed for the good of the organization, *and the good of the larger organization must always take precedence over individual recovery.*

---

[8] Of course, the exceptions are the ones who make the six o'clock news. When Terry Murray was CEO of Fleet Bank during its infamous Fleet Focus downsizing a decade ago, he called in his own brother-in-law to tell him personally that he was no longer an officer—nor an employee—of the bank. I'm sure that subsequent Christmas parties were interesting in the Murray household.

Case Study

The Catholic Church became embroiled in controversy, poor publicity, and lawsuits that threatened the existence of some archdiocese when pedophilia committed by priests was proved. The ensuing problems were not solely the result of these tragic occurrences—after all, the vast preponderance of the clergy constitute dedicated, holy, ethical people who are exemplars of the faith—but rather by the proven cover-up of the crimes by some members of the Church hierarchy.

The bishops, who are actually the executives or general managers of the organization, who moved the transgressors and did not take punitive actions, damaged the repute and standing of the entire organization in order to try to rehabilitate or save a few. This was an unfortunate but perfect example of the harm that befalls organizations when individual failings are not directly, candidly, ethically, and uniformly addressed.

It is not unusual—in fact, in my experience it's rather common—to find in the course of a consulting assignment that someone is lax, incompetent, uncaring, untrained, unethical, or generally asleep at the switch. I never ignore them. I report them to the proper, accountable manager and provide evidence and observed behavior. If that manager is my buyer, I follow up to instigate action, *because I owe that to the buyer.*

My philosophy is simple: People who are not performing should be trained, educated, and otherwise developed to perform at proper levels. If they cannot be for whatever reason, they should be transferred to a job they can perform well in. If that is not possible or unacceptable, they should be terminated. This dynamic obtains whether the performance problem is competence based (they don't know how to perform) or attitude based (they choose not to perform), and it is applicable across geographic, gender, compensation, ethnic, racial, cultural, hierarchical, and functional lines. A female vice president in the corporate office should perform up to or beyond her job require-

> The failure to make tough calls on performance—be they based on competence or volition—is the Achilles' heel of internal consulting. If you don't rock the boat, it will never break free of the mud. Waiting for high tide in a pond is like leaving the landing lights on for Amelia Earhart—a nice gesture, but ultimately futile.

ments just as a male salesperson in the field should perform up to or beyond his.

The acceptance of poor performance without remedial attempts to correct it and without consequences if it is uncorrected is one of the greatest detriments to productivity and performance in corporate America. It is a plague on firms, nonprofits, charities, community groups, trade associations, and all other forms of organizational life.

You may find poor performance in conditions such as:

✔ Poor supervision has created inadequate training of front-line people.

✔ Changed conditions have made past practices—however well performed—inappropriate and inadequate. (Try to maintain a data base without a computer.)

✔ Turf battles and private agendas create deliberate noncooperation at best and sabotage at worst.

✔ Weak leadership thwarts innovation and creates an atmosphere of "keep your head down and do nothing."

✔ Poor communication skills create uncertainty, fear, and/or misdirection.

✔ Vague or unreasonable goals undermine common and uniform market approaches and decision making.

✔ High turnover reduces selection quality and training quantity.

Your job is to confront these weaknesses head-on. As a general manager at Merck told me once as we strode through his division, "If I see people underperforming, I seek out their manager and make whatever improvements or changes are needed. That's where the accountability is. No one should be underperforming and be unmolested and uninvolved in improvement."

That confrontation takes courage, but why work in an environment that doesn't prize such boldness? If you don't confront and attempt to resolve these performance problems—at any level and under any conditions—then you, yourself, are underperforming and become a part of the problem rather than the solution.

A cynic told me once that a consultant was someone brought in to study a problem who then stayed on to become a part of it. Unfortunately, that is often the truth in internal consulting.

When working with a large insurance company, I found that the vice president of sales—a powerful person generally feared by even his colleagues—was actually accountable for severe ethical lapses in the field, which had created the highly unwelcome attention of the state insurance commissioner. The vice president had encouraged almost any practice to obtain business, and his sales force was all to eager too please him.

During a senior management meeting on ethics convened by the CEO and facilitated by me, I asked about "right, wrong, and gray areas" of conduct. "They're all gray," said the vice president, "and we have to interpret them."

"Surely," I said to a deadly quiet room, "there are cases where the line in the sand is quite clear."

"I don't think so," he said dismissively.

"What about an agent forging the name of a potential customer on the application?" I asked, referring to three actual cases we had found of this illegal and unethical practice.

"Sometimes you have to do what you have to do," he said.

The room took a collective intake of air, and the CEO stood to inform the vice president and everyone else within earshot that such practices were not acceptable and were subject to immediate termination. We went on to list what was "right, wrong, and gray," and the gray area was quite small.

The vice president apologized to the group the next morning, and his reign of terror was over. A colleague of his told me that the actual practices weren't surprising, since everyone had really known about them, but the fact that no one internally had had the courage to confront him about them was shocking. How was I able to do it? he wondered.

"It's what I'm paid to do," I explained.

It's what we're all paid to do.

SUGGESTED READING

Not Just for CEOs by Jack Zenger (Irwin, 1996). Jack Zenger was a human resources director who left his high-tech, Silicon Valley job to launch Zenger-Miller, a highly successful training and development firm, ultimately purchased by the Times Mirror Corporation. He's an intelligent, honest, and insightful practitioner who provides excellent techniques in this short book that stands CEOs and everyone else in good stead. I'd suggest also reading its companion, *Making 2 + 2 = 5* (Irwin, 1996), which features still more pragmatic ideas about how to act in an objective, effective, and professional manner despite what's going on around you.

Chapter

Knowing When to Stop

How to Disengage, Give Credit, and (It's Allowed) Take Credit

ASSESSING PROGRESS AND COMPLETION

The earlier focus on conceptual agreement (objectives/ measures/value) plays an important role in knowing when and how to disengage. Disengagement is as important as the engagement.

Without a crisp and clear ending point you run these risks:

✔ Eventually something will go wrong, and you will be blamed.

✔ You'll be regarded as a permanent fixture in support of the project.

✔ Your time will disappear into the maw of open-ended projects.

✔ You'll be deemed accountable for long-term reinforcement, rather than your client's own people.

✔ Scope creep will inevitably descend, and you'll be asked to work on "related" issues, which aren't related at all except for being under the same roof.

173

The key to reaching the completion point is emphasizing progress checkpoints. Many consultants achieve this by using "deliverables" as indications of motion: The workshops were taught, the report was submitted, the system was set up, the clients were canvassed. But I don't like tasks and inputs (which is all that deliverables really are) as the progress indicators, since they can all be met *without the client's objectives being met.* Just because you train the entire call center staff in new phone techniques doesn't mean that sales have increased, and just because you've submitted a report, it doesn't automatically follow that cross-functional collaboration has been enhanced one iota.

The metrics, ideally, should indicate sales improvement, retention enhancement, customer satisfaction growth, and so on. These are *business outcomes* which warm the cockles of any buyer's heart. This is why the silly "four levels of measurement" alluded to earlier is useless. No one will remember you for the fact that people liked your course, scored well on a test, or claim a "new attitude." "Show me the money," Cuba Gooding tells Tom Cruise in the film *Jerry McGuire.* "Show me the results" is what every buyer is entitled to demand of us.

> The metrics established before beginning the project will enable you to successfully end the project. But unless they measure changed results in the environment, you might as well be writing an esoteric college thesis back in your office.

During the course of a consulting project, here is the discipline you should employ to ensure that you reach a successful disengagement point:

Meet with the Buyer Regularly. Establish a personal meeting schedule, even if it's for 20 minutes, face-to-face. (This is something external consultants have difficulty achieving, since they don't live there and meetings must be painfully scheduled.) At the outset of a project, this should be weekly. As the project unfolds, you can reduce it to bi-weekly. But do not allow that contact to become any less frequent. In the worst case (travel, other sites, full schedules), do it by phone (e-mail is not interactive and not sufficient).

Deliver Good News. Too many buyer meetings occur only to discuss implementation problems. Use these meetings to keep the buyer abreast of positive developments and progress. That way, when you do have to deliver the inevitable news about delays and foot-dragging, it will be in perspective and in proportion to the constructive progress being made.

Make These Interactive. Ask the buyer his or her reactions to your progress report. Ask whether this is better or worse than envisioned. Ask if there are any refinements needed. If the buyer must take action (e.g., light a fire under a lagging subordinate) then set up a time to follow up on that accountability. Remember that this is a *partnership* and not a superior/subordinate relationship.

Document the Discussion. I don't like to send anything in writing in advance (largely because this diminishes the importance of the dialogue and may even prompt the buyer to say the report is sufficient and cancel the meeting). Far better is to send a hard copy summary of the discussion, *including any agreed upon action points and accountabilities for each of you*, following the meeting, and use that document as a discussion topic for the ensuing meeting. These summaries keep things moving forward and demonstrate progress.

Err by Overcommunicating. I've learned that it's virtually impossible to communicate too much during a project. Give your buyer the option of ignoring or filing unneeded information, but don't do the buyer the injustice of censoring the information beforehand. Send e-mail, notes, and phone messages between your regular meetings as needed. If, for example, you had agreed to interview a key department head whose cooperation was needed, leave a voice mail message indicating that the meeting took place and that cooperation was promised.

Of course, very seldom will progress be as smooth as a jog around the park. You're going to encounter tough terrain, dogs on the loose, poor weather, broken sidewalks, and the occasional mugger. In assessing progress, you have to be brutally honest with the buyer, so that these hazards, which come with the turf, can be realistically appraised and overcome. You'll almost always need the buyer's clout to help you to do this, which is why the *partnership* aspect of the project is so important.

> The default position in the face of poor or no communication is always bad, because the field is left to rumors, innuendo, and the undermining by the inevitably unhappy people who would prefer to see the change effort fail. Do not surrender this field to the enemy.

Problems need to be identified and dealt with as soon as possible in order to keep the project on its time frames. Apprise the buyer immediately of even suspected resistance or opposition. Don't try to smooth things over and pretend that everyone is on board. First, that seldom is ever the case. Second, the buyer will accept this (Who wouldn't accept good news in a busy day?) uncritically, and will later demand, when things are seriously wrong, to know why you hadn't spotted the trouble earlier. That's not a position that builds your credibility or leverage.

With rare exceptions, I've seen few projects—even those that are organization wide and profound in their change—that take more than six to nine months to implement. You must keep a tight rein on the time frames and deadlines within them. My rule is to try to collapse time frames—make project implementation as rapid as possible—even though buyers often feel gradual approaches are less disruptive.

Basically, that is a false premise. The longer project implementation takes, the more the risk of:

✔ Unrelated events (competitive moves, the economy, other priorities) affecting the project.

✔ Key people and resources becoming unavailable (transfers, resignations, disruptions).

Case Study

Working with the president of a billion dollar division of a pharmaceutical company, I apprised him of the fact that several of his direct reports clearly were providing lip service to our project but were actually vigorously opposing it in reality. He correctly pointed out that it would be counterproductive to try to take up the issue based on my word against theirs, so I suggested a more objective test.

We scheduled a meeting, during which the president took a position that was slightly cynical and directly questioned some of my suggestions. The vice presidents I had warned him about jumped to the bait like starving trout, and erupted with dozens of reasons why the project made no sense and should be scrapped.

The president was convinced about what I had described, and worked one-on-one with each of the recalcitrant reports so as not to publicly embarrass them, but to make clear that the project would commence, preferably with them, but even without them.

That was the turning point of that project, and wouldn't have been achieved without the relationship that the president and I had developed.

- ✔ The opposition gathering more leverage as they rally unhappy people.
- ✔ The pain of the change is prolonged while the salutary effects of the change are delayed, distorting the dynamics of what was once a positive force field.
- ✔ Your buyer becomes bored, jaded, or unavailable.
- ✔ The more your own time is either compromised by other projects or is unavailable for other projects (both undesirable conditions).

✔ The less you are able to demonstrate short-term ROI for your project, thereby endangering its future.

The moral is, don't just assess progress, but make every attempt to accelerate it. The metrics are established to be exceeded, not merely satisfied. You haven't achieved anything by implementing a project, nor by managing it. You've only achieved something when you've completed it and walked away from a happy buyer.

MAKING A CLEAN BREAK

It's tougher to make a clean break as an internal consultant if you're "living with" your client. (Of course, it's easier when you're from another site entirely.[1]) But it's nonetheless important.

The reasons for a clean break (e.g., no lingering loose ends to tie up, no ongoing client expectations, a formal "ciao," etc.) include:

✔ Transition of any remaining implementation to the client and an end (not merely a reduction) to your support for this.

✔ Ongoing monitoring and accountability now fully rest with the client.

✔ Future calls upon you will mean a new proposal and new agreements.

✔ Your time must be allocated elsewhere.

✔ It must be demonstrated that the project can self-perpetuate and live without life support.

✔ Your own growth, health, and happiness will not be fulfilled, and you can't reach out to new projects without letting go of what you currently manage.

---

[1]While not a topic for this book, internal consultants who work in remote sites from time to time are sometimes more like external consultants, or at least hybrids, than strictly internal consultants. For targeted advice on how to work in those conditions, see my books *Process Consultation* (Jossey-Bass/Pfeiffer, 2002) for implementation advice, and *How to Acquire Clients* (Jossey-Bass/Pfeiffer, 2002) for marketing help. Both are part of the seven-book series *The Ultimate Consultant*.

> There is only one place to go from the pedestal, and that is downward at 32 feet per second, squared. Go out on top, and don't linger, like those ex-jocks who hung around the high school even after they had been graduated. They went from heroes as seniors to pathetic as graduates who couldn't let go.

Ironically, the more effective you are sometimes, the less the client wants to let go, so you need a formal system in order to pry the buyer's fingers from around your neck. Many consultants are so flattered by the attention and requests for continuance, that they blithely (and blinded by ego) agree, and the relationship usually deteriorates from there, because you've already hit your peak with that project and that buyer.

Here are the somewhat surprising steps for creating a clean disengagement from any project that is successful:

Begin the Process about 80 Percent of the Way through the Project. The worst thing you can do is to show up in the buyer's office and say, "What weather, huh? And, oh, by the way, we're done." Begin to lay the groundwork when you can see the finish line in the distance. For example:

- ✔ In your regular meetings, cite the date when you believe the project will be complete insofar as your involvement is concerned. (Don't forget, this should have been specified in the proposal, so there's no surprise here.)
- ✔ Cite the metrics that indicate progress is significant and almost to the expected end point for the project phase.
- ✔ Ask if the buyer is prepared to implement the transition plan, and whether all accountabilities are in place.
- ✔ Specify that you'll be available by phone and e-mail for questions, but that your presence and personal involvement will otherwise be ending, per agreement.
- ✔ As always, summarize this in writing.

Create the Transition Team. You've been personally providing support, answering questions, being a cheerleader, interceding with management, and so on. Create a team from the stakeholders who are accountable for these duties. Make yourself available to them for an interim period after you leave (e.g., 30 days maximum).

> You are most professional and most successful when your name is no longer associated with the project. The only thing that matters is that the buyer is fully aware that it couldn't have been done without you. Consultants bank return engagements, not ego.

Find and Support at Least Two Key Sponsors. Identify two executives, senior managers, sales experts, union leaders—anyone with organizational respect who will continue to clearly lend their credibility to the project. Unlike at the outset, by this time the success will have created significant appeal for people to want to take on the credit for continued leadership.

I suggest two people because one may disappear in ordinary organizational life (transfer, vacation, relocation, promotion, departure, illness, shifting priorities, etc.), and too many will dilute the credit aspect and the focus of accountability. (The buyer is always a third sponsor in the picture, anyway.) Unlike the transition teams, which provide tactical and operational support, the sponsors provide motivational support and clout if needed.

Ensure that All Knowledge Resources Are in Place. It's always going to be easier to call you and ask a question, so you must mitigate this need by arranging for alternative and simple support processes. I've found the most effective, and the easiest, include:

✔ Web-based interactive help, including most frequently asked questions, self-paced learning, and constantly updated best practices examples.

✔ Regular feedback and response to the transition team.

✔ Phone and e-mail hot lines for stakeholder questions.

✔ Simple manuals and job aids, which can sit on a desk and be easily accessed (not unlike quick start guides you get with otherwise complex computer and cable software).

✔ Scheduled focus groups and/or interviews with employees and customers to continue to sample progress, perception, and suggestions.

Hold a Formal Departure Activity. Visit your key contacts and shake hands, signifying that your formal involvement is now over. Present everyone with a small memento from the project. Submit a final report to the buyer. Clear out your desk, cubicle, or office if you were using space on site. Terminate any special e-mail, voice mail, or other communications links that were created for you during the project. Go to lunch with your closest collaborators.

Case Study

I've had clients who created a myriad of devices to overcome the fact that I'm external to the organization: special voice mail boxes tied to the client's system; a special internal e-mail address; administrative support; a fixed home base location; identification and pass cards to breeze past security points; parking space; cafeteria privileges; even my own coffee cup!

Once the project is complete, I never worry about terminating all that, because a client contact diligently collects, unhooks, confiscates, and otherwise repossesses all of it. (I usually get to keep the coffee cup.)

As an internal person, you already have some of the amenities, but may also receive situational additional ones. It's a good idea to terminate all those extra "perks" as if you were an outsider like me. If you can no longer get past security or literally open a particular door, your involvement is effectively over!

You get the idea. Engage in some rituals that clearly signal "This is the end of my involvement. *Sayonara.*" Culturally, this sends one of the strongest signals that you have moved on, and it's a tangible and professional practice.

To summarize, establish your clean break well before it actually occurs—first by stipulating certain facts and expectations in the original proposal, then by preparing the buyer well in advance, and finally by ensuring that your termination plan is in place, staffed, and functional.

Those overflowing folders on desks and credenzas and the voice mail and e-mail messages piled 10 deep are indicative of a consultant who cannot or will not turn off the spigot. I don't know how many projects you can handle at one time—that depends on their nature, your energy, and your resources—but I do know that you can't continue to handle every one you've ever worked on. Sooner or later everything collapses and, worse, current work suffers from lingering past work.

> If you don't disengage from the past, you'll have a hard time working in the present. But, worse, as a consultant, you'll have no future.

Disengagement, therefore, is as important as engagement. You must know how to start, how to deliver, and how to end. Failure in any of the three areas is a disservice to your buyer and a weakness in your professionalism.

If you don't have a map, calendar, flow chart, or some other instrument visible with your project starting dates *and ending dates*, then you're not serious about managing your business and serving your constituency. Consultants who work on relatively few projects a year—and who, therefore, are not providing much ROI for their organizations—are neither overworked nor overwhelmed.

They simply won't let go.

CLOSING THE LOOP WITH THE BUYER

You've developed an important and valuable relationship, and at this point you've proven that you can deliver what you promise. That sequence is absolutely basic to highly successful consulting. To me, it looks like Figure 9.1.

The results of a successful implementation reinforce the relationship. This is the apotheosis of successful partnering with line buyers—you've worked with them to achieve a predicted, positive future. You've improved the client's condition, just as you promised.

The value to you of that heightened relationship may be manifest in:

✔ Future projects.
✔ Referrals to other buyers.

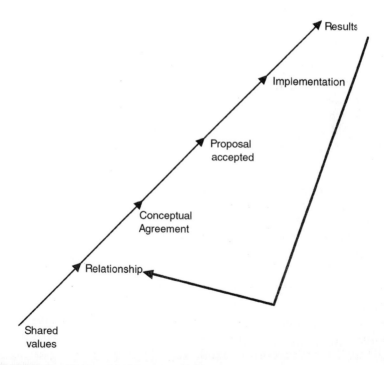

FIGURE 9.1 Core consulting sequence

✔ Promotion and support within the organization.

✔ A heightened repute and credibility.

✔ The buyer's serving as a mentor in the future.

✔ Your serving as a mentor to the buyer in the future.

✔ Your ability to take stronger, even controversial positions.

> Engagements end, but relationships should be enduring. Unfortunately, many consultants believe that ending one also ends the other. There's a difference, however, between what you do and whom you know.

Inexplicably, both external and internal consultants often (usually?) forsake the relationship when they disengage from the project. I've never understood this. Project should end, but relationships should endure. This means that closing the loop with the buyer is *a perpetuating technique, not a termination technique.*

There are two dimensions involved in closing the loop with your buyer, one project related and the other relationship related. Here are the hallmarks.

Project Conclusion

The buyer should be formally and clearly aware that the project has been successfully implemented (improvement made, problem eliminated, condition altered, etc.). He or she should know who on the staff is accountable for further reinforcement and fine-tuning, including the buyer's own accountabilities and sponsorship. The buyer should have an undisturbed and sufficient opportunity to ask any remaining questions and be apprised of what to expect from this point onward, including your involvement or lack of involvement. ("Your people can always call with questions, but I won't be accompanying them any more on client visits.")

Relationship Perpetuation

The relationship between you and the buyer should be continued, albeit on some modified bases. But you should make it clear that you are expecting some continued interaction, and demonstrate reasons for that expectation. There is a thin line between hanging around and haunting a busy executive *and* assuming a position of ongoing help and support.

The entire proposition here is based on which direction the value is flowing. In other words, if the buyer perceives that you are intent on hanging on to some coattails or getting an inside track on more work, your presence will not be appreciated. But if you are methodically and judiciously providing value, you will be seen as a resource.

Relationships are perpetuated by consultants—and, again, internal

---

Case Study

An internal consultant assigned to my team had boasted—and I believed with justification—of an assignment two years prior during which she had helped reorganize the financial reporting procedures to make them much more useful to the operating divisions. It was clear to me that in six months she had probably helped the company make an invaluable transition.

At a meeting during which the senior management team was present to hear of our project's plans and their role in supporting a new customer service protocol, the vice president of finance twice called my internal colleague by the wrong name and mentioned that he hoped this project was as successful as the financial reporting procedures was for him, which he claimed had been implemented by the firm's external auditors.

After the meeting, she sheepishly said, "How quickly they forget." I asked her what her involvement had been with her former buyer post-project. "This was only the third time I've been in a room with him since then," she admitted.

consultants have a tremendous advantage in this arena by dint of physical presence—through one or more of the following techniques:

✔ Arrange periodic follow-up or audit meetings. Plan a formal meeting with the buyer once every 60 days or so to review progress.

✔ Create "best practices." Use the buyer's project as a basis for best practices for other operations, and reciprocate by regularly providing the buyer with best practices from elsewhere.

If you've worked in an organization on change initiatives and/or consulting projects for more than a year, and don't have at least three or four senior managers who are part of your ongoing relationship network, you have either ignored their importance or executed poor projects. Either condition is fatal to your future.

✔ Respond to the buyer's personal interests. You may find a sport, hobby, subject matter, or other item of interest in your dealings, which you can continue to support and communicate about. I helped one buyer with information about the region in which his daughter had chosen to attend college, and we communicated for four years about her progress and experiences.

✔ Create a communications mechanism. You might use an e-mail newsletter of two paragraphs that goes out on the first of each month with "tips for change." You may drop by the buyer's office regularly with an article or other resource. Maybe you can jog together at lunch once a week. Find an excuse to talk and exchange views.

✔ Ask the buyer to serve on a mutually-beneficial panel or body. He or she might be a part of your review team for new orientation techniques, or play a role in assessing the merit of employee grievances. Choose something that is not time-consuming but is prestigious.

When you close the loop you are concurrently ending a project and continuing a relationship. The buyer's natural tendency may be to assume that both end together (especially if you've been scrupulous about avoiding scope creep and other demands on your time). Begin to dissuade the buyer of that view at the same time you prepare the buyer for the disengagement—well before the actual end of the project.

BLOWING YOUR OWN HORN

Most consultants in my experience have difficulty claiming credit. Strangely, there are many who sweat and labor over their assignments, take all blame for setback and reversal even when factors are beyond their influence, and then collapse in gratitude over a successful project completion as though just having completed a marathon.

That's a crazy way to engage in one's chosen profession.

Braggadocio and vanity shouldn't be part of the concert. But there's nothing wrong in taking pride in the way you play. After all, when you're a one-person band, if you don't blow your own horn, there is no music.

It's wrong to suffer the sometimes deserved and sometimes undeserved brickbats thrown at the profession and not to bask in the glow of professional success. Consulting is a noble profession and shouldn't demand martyrdom. ("Don't pity the martyrs," said humorist George Ade. "They love the work.")

The question isn't "Should I accept credit for my role in the success?" but rather "*How* should I accept credit for my role in the success?" The objective is unequivocal; it's the tactics that are tricky.

Yet you must claim some credit and take visible accolades for a successfully completed project.

Alan's 10 Reasons for Claiming Credit and Accepting Applause

1. No one else will do this on your behalf. Others will tend to downplay your role, particularly if people wonder why "This never happened before" and ask "What took so long?"

2. Others will be quick to claim credit. I'm not talking about the buyer, but rather underlings who see the opportunity to parlay their participation at some meetings into the guiding forces for the entire initiative.

3. Absence does not make the heart grow fonder. Despite an ongoing relationship with the buyer (or, worse, if you've failed to maintain one) people will honestly forget external help. Many consultants know their projects have become most totally and effectively integrated when their names are no longer associated with the change.

4. You need "marketing" within the organization. Internal consultants are less able to aggressively market than external consultants, except for the most effective marketing approach of all: word-of-mouth and referrals. While the project is hot and results dramatic, your value is significantly enhanced.

5. This is a career opportunity. If you have desires for advancement into line management, other divisions, and/or other functions entirely, this is the way to build your resume.

6. Overcome the bad press that otherwise arises. The default position for human resources, training, and other change agent functions in many organizations is negative. Whether merited or not, this is an effective countervailing force to change perceptions.

7. You are being evaluated. Presumably, your merit increases, bonuses, incentive, and other perks rely to a great degree on our consulting success, and it's far better for the project's success to speak loudly than for your own superior, who may not be intimately aware of your contributions, to do this across a sterile conference table.

8. You'll set an example. Your colleagues should be performing in the manner you are, and this will encourage them to use your consulting approaches, build the same kind of relationships, and claim credit in the same manner. You'll be building a critical mass and serving as the exemplar.

9. You will draw people to you. One of the most powerful aspects of leadership—which does not require hierarchical power or appointment—is "referent," meaning that people seek you out and follow your advice *because they believe in your competency and sincerity.* You can become a powerful, informal organizational leader.

10. Your ego deserves it. If we suffer in the troughs of life and work, we deserve to exult in the peaks and apogees. There's nothing wrong with some modest and appropriate celebration of victory.

Special Reason 11: In an age of downsizing, layoffs, and irrational draconian cuts, the more obviously valuable you are to the organization, the harder it is to arbitrarily terminate your employment. Think about it— human resources operations are hit very hard, or simply outsourced in totality, because the organization perceives no great inherent value in maintaining the expense. It's up to you to turn your work into a highly visible asset if you want to gain employment security and a sound sleep.

Success begins eponymously as "Alan's project." Then it becomes "Alan's help." Then we move to "The Project." Next it's "Call Alan if we need him," which becomes, "Do we need Alan?" Success ends with "We've had great results, and we didn't even need Alan on this one!"

How to claim credit without looking boastful, incurring the wrath of others, and being deemed a public nuisance? There are ways, fortunately.

No one succeeds by merely correcting weaknesses. We must grow based on our strengths. This also means that we can't focus solely on failures, but must understand and exploit our successes. So you need a plan to capitalize on victories, just as you needed a plan to implement your project. Organizations are political entities, and I state that not as a critique but merely as a fact. Knowing that to be true, we are negligent if we're not prepared to deal with that aspect of our environment.

Here are some ideas to apply to blowing your own horn to create music that everyone begins to hum along with. You can apply them all, or be selective, but *plan to do something*.

Ask Permission to Use the Buyer for a Reference. This simple tactic will often gain you entry immediately into other projects where the buyers are peers of your existing buyer.

Ask for Referrals. Once you've proved your worth, ask, "Are there other parts of the company where I could be assisting in this same manner and, if so, could you provide me with an introduction?"[2]

Write about It Internally. Most organizations have house organs that welcome good news and good examples of successful corporate initiatives. There might also be an intranet or other communications device where posting the results—always with the permission of the buyer—will be effective.

Write about It Externally. Sometimes you can get permission to write up your work as a case study for a magazine, newsletter, consulting journal, or other source. You can then circulate those reprints internally. (Hint: If you can get your line buyer or key stakeholders to collaborate on the article, you enhance the chances of both internal approval and external publishing.)

Create Best Practices. Establish the work and its methodology—from acquisition through disengagement—as a "best practice" and

---

[2]Again, I believe that it's a dangerous misconception to view internal consulting as a reactive role. It becomes most vibrant and best perceived when it is assertively marketed and thrust into existing plans.

provide it for people to emulate, both within the consulting operation and within the line organizations (if they're able to do it on their own). This is a very effective way to thwart external competition. ("We've done this before, there is precedent internally, so why hire outside people?")

Talk about It Formally. Include examples in presentations you're asked to conduct. Cite the work, in whole or in part, to emphasize how successful change initiatives are implemented.

Talk about It Informally. Unless you're under a rare internal nondisclosure agreement (much more common for external consultants and another internal advantage), cite your experience conversationally. This needn't be in an immodest fashion, but more in an informative manner. In other words, keep your name associated with the success.

> With a string of victories to your credit, you will have effectively reversed all prior momentum, and you'll be credited with more than you deserve. Don't worry a whole lot about correcting this misconception.

Create a Portfolio

Very few internal consultants do this, but there's good reason to create a "portfolio"—sort of an internal brochure—that cites the projects you've worked on and the salutary results. This might be an individual undertaking, contained in a three-ring binder, or a departmental project, in four-color and duplicated on your intranet site. Who says that internal consultants can't create a marketing brochure? Wouldn't this be an important asset to place before a new buyer, with dubious beliefs, wondering whether or not you can really be of help? I'm always surprised that more internal people don't take advantage of such approaches.

Since I believe in concurrent and overlapping projects, you should be adept at blowing your own horn as a matter of fact, since the formal time to do so will not arise if you're successfully engaged in a variety of projects in varied states of progress. And, ironically perhaps, you will most likely be fully engaged (and, therefore, fully employed) when you are matter-of-factly manifesting the credit you deserve for joint successes.

SUGGESTED READING

A Guide to Tactical Planning: Producing Your Short-Term Results by George Morrissey (Jossey-Bass, 1996). This author is the master of planning (his *Morrissey on Planning* series also includes strategy and long-range planning). This particular book will tell you everything that a line manager needs (and, hence, you need) to know about implementing a plan, whether for your client or your own success as a consultant.

PART FOUR

THE AFTERMATH

Assessing Value

How to Follow-Up and Leverage Your Success

DEVELOPING YOUR SKILLS

It's no accident that we find ourselves back in a marketing position, sort of full circle, in the aftermath of a project completion. Salespeople search for new prospects; R&D people experiment to find new products and applications; financial people seek new cost savings and economies; internal change agents should be looking for new clients.

Why should your role be a passive one when everyone else is assertive and searching?

The wonderful cycle of consulting success means that you are engaged to help a client, which adds to your learning; that improved learning makes you of increased value; that increased value makes you more attractive to the next client, who engages you to learn still more.

As you can see in Figure 10.1, we can enter into a wonderful cycle of learning, value, more learning, more value. This is a dynamic that is rare—doctors, lawyers, accountants, and other professionals rarely enter into it. I think that architects, directors, and others involved in the arts come closest.

There is no body of knowledge in the consulting profession, such

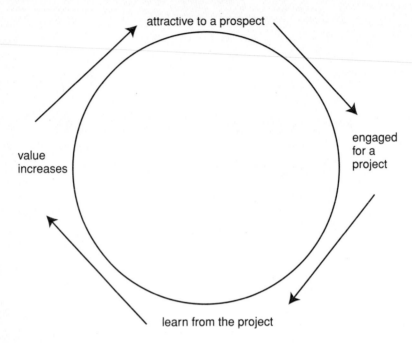

FIGURE 10.1   The consultant value cycle

as there is in law or accounting, nor is there a certificate, license, or charter that must be obtained before we can hang out our shingle. That applies to external and internal consultants. Consulting is really advice, and there are no parameters or paradigms for advice and counsel, other than in the psychology profession, where there are structured protocols for helping patients.

If you read diligently the works of Howard Shenson, Herman Holtz, Peter Block, and mine—a total of scores of books from the peo-

> If you haven't learned anything from a project, then you've failed and just don't realize it, no matter what the buyer might say. Your job requires continual self-development and, fortunately, it usually comes with the turf if we allow it to.

ple who have written more about consulting in the past two decades than anyone else—you would be unable to come up with a common body of knowledge or procedures other than the common sense parameters of legal and ethical propriety. The largest national professional association for individual consultants, the Institute of Management Consultants, has a small minority of active consultants as members and is a relatively weak body in terms of influence on the profession. The largest and best organized group for internal consultants, the consultants special interest group of the Society for Human Resource Management, is active and respected, but also has very little influence on the roles, conduct, and standards for the profession.

The good and bad news is that the learning in this business is largely the responsibility of the individual practitioner, on the job. If you've completed a project, therefore (successful or otherwise), here is a template to help ensure that the individual learning and continual development of higher value propositions perpetuates. I hope you'll feel free to copy this and use it immediately on current and approaching projects.

The Self-Development Template

1. Did the project meet, fail to meet, or exceed the objectives established?
2. What are the main reasons for that result?
3. What, if anything, should I have done differently to have improved the outcome?
4. In what areas, if any, did I have to request help that shouldn't have been necessary (I should have been able to handle it myself)?
5. What were my greatest learning points in each of these areas?

   ✔ New skills or new application of existing skills.
   ✔ New knowledge or new application of existing knowledge.
   ✔ New behavior or new application of existing behavior.
   ✔ New experience.
   ✔ New relationship.

6. How, specifically, will I use these learning points systematically in future projects?

7. What weaknesses emerged, if any, which I must correct and how will I correct them?

8. What resources do I need to include, access, or utilize better in the future to add to my value?

9. How will I manifest these new talents and abilities to existing and potential buyers?

10. Using what I've learned, how can I more aggressively market my talents and ability to help clients?

Tools for change: The 1% Solution™ states that if you improve by 1 percent a day, in 70 days, you're twice as good. Yet not many people achieve that, because they don't take responsibility for improvement into their own hands. As consultants, we have no choice if we want to succeed.

This assessment is equally useful for projects that succeeded wildly, met the objectives mundanely, or crashed in flames. The key is to learn, not always to win.

In fact, here's a deep secret that not many consultants ever talk about: If you haven't failed, you're not growing. None of us—who're any good—have a perfect record. By taking risks, stretching, and seeking out more and more challenging projects, we are bound to fail at some junctures. Anyone who claims they haven't is in one of three conditions: They've never tried anything risky; they've failed and just don't know it; or they're lying.

We're not in this to stick our toe into the water; we're in this to make waves. The more we learn, the larger the waves. I don't know about you, but I'm not motivated too much any longer by projects to improve morale in the call center. What turns me on are the projects to redesign succession planning, merge uncommon cultures, or align individual objectives behind corporate goals. The beauty of being a consultant is that, unlike a trainer, you can remain involved to see the results of your change efforts.

And the beauty of being *an internal consultant* is that you also get to live with those results on a permanent basis.

DEVELOPING OTHER BUYERS

If we keep in mind the "value cycle" in Figure 10.1, we can begin to develop additional business. Remember that a "fully employed," highly valued consultant is not only leading a more fulfilling and productive corporate life, but is also gaining immunity against every adverse condition from termination at one end to unpleasant assignments at the other.

One of the reasons that HR has been such an easy target for outsourcing and cost reductions is that *it has sat there like a lump, seldom taking the pains to manifest value assertively.* "We're here if you need us" is hardly a compelling reason to develop great affinity for any organization, except maybe the local fire house.

> If you disappeared for a week, would anyone notice? I'm quite serious. Does it make a difference to the organization and to colleagues whether you are involved or not? It's best to ask that question of yourself privately, in a small room with a large drink.

The cardinal rule for any consultant, internal or external, is to capitalize on and exploit success. This catapults us forward as well as mitigating the inevitable setbacks that we encounter along the way. Some sources will advise you to sit back and rest upon your laurels, awaiting the next call to action. Follow that advice, and you'll find yourself and your laurels resting in the street. *This is the consulting profession, but it's also the marketing business.*

Developing new buyers is a process of assertive networking.

Figure 10.2 shows how an external consultant might aggressively network his or her current success.

In the example, our friends at Acme reach out to critical hubs of extended relationships—clients, media, trade associations, speaking opportunities—to utilize the "reach" of those sources for still further networking (to vendors, readers, advertisers, etc.).

An internal consultant might not have these sources or opportunities, you're thinking, but the point is that the *process* works, and we merely have to include slightly different content. Figure 10.3 shows one example of how the interrelationships might appear to a successful, internal consultant.

Note that I've included only two current buyers. You may have more than two, and you probably have a dozen past buyers (assuming you've retained the relationships as discussed earlier) you can add to the chart. "Vendors" appear because many organizations demand that their key suppliers adopt the same efficiencies and meth-

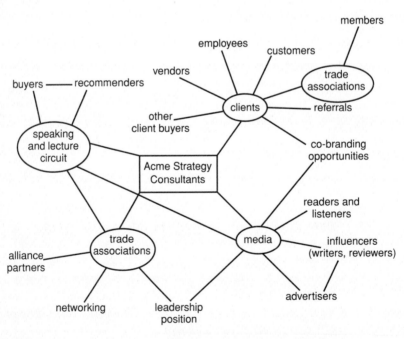

FIGURE 10.2 Assertive networking for an external consultant

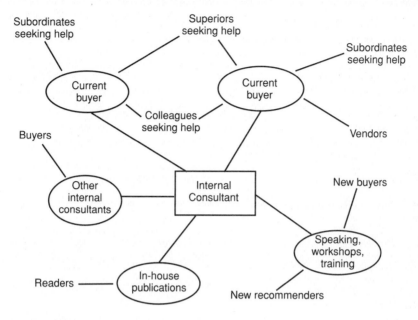

FIGURE 10.3 The internal network potential

ods being used in the buying organization in areas including quality, ethics, customer service, and so on. In many cases, the buying organization is willing to provide the consulting and training expertise to help launch such initiatives. I haven't included still other sources that may be unique to your organization, such as a widely-used intranet capability.

Among delivering your services, networking for new clients, maintaining past relationships, and focusing on continual self-development, the internal consultant should have a very full schedule and a very important role in organizational life. Why, then, are so many sitting around waiting for the phone to ring or engaging in projects such as how to improve the bulletin boards?

When you attempt to develop new business for yourself, *always* bear in mind that we should be focusing on output, not input. It's not what we do, but how the client is helped that's important. This may prompt you to change your conversation, claims, and choreography.

For example, in the following lists the left column lists what most internal consultants and HR departments tend to talk about and promote. The right column lists what buyers really need.

What's Highlighted	*What's Needed*
✔ Training and workshops.	✔ Talent acquisition and retention.
✔ 360° assessments.	✔ Effective leadership.
✔ Compensation and benefits.	✔ Succession planning.
✔ Employee/customer surveys.	✔ Alignment of objectives/incentive.
✔ Focus groups.	✔ Customer satisfaction/ repeat sales.
✔ Improved communications.	✔ Faster response time.
✔ Team building.	✔ Cross-functional collaboration.
✔ Behavioral/personality testing.	✔ Coaching/counseling/ mentoring.
✔ Diversity awareness.	✔ Ethical conduct.
✔ Games and simulations.	✔ Improved profits.
✔ Use of technology.	✔ Knowledge management.
✔ Access to external resources.	✔ Superb on-site resources.

If I've been unfair to your department or your focus, mea culpa. The point I want to drill home is that *developing new buyers requires that you think, speak, and act as those buyers do.* No one in a line position cares about right-brain thinking, personality tests, empowerment, or open meetings. If those are vehicles to gain results, fine (although that's highly dubious), but the results are what count.

You can't align yourself as a purveyor of patent oils and healing balms. In fact, one of the very worst occurrences in any organization—

one that I'm often called in to fix—is when a senior manager becomes enamored with a flavor of the month intervention, and suddenly everyone has to have their ticket stamped in the MBTI course, or the brain hemisphere workshop, or the cycle sales system. When internal people jump on these ephemeral and ineffective bandwagons, they suffer the same eventual ignominy of the approach: They are discredited and often disappear. (Many a senior executive has been flushed away through the zealous demand that the troops all experience a favored crazy intervention once it came to the attention of shareholders or public regulatory authorities.)

> If you focus on results with new buyers, you can't possibly miss the mark, because you're talking their language. There is no need for interpretation and you will immediately share common objectives.

My moral: Don't embark on an ultimately futile journey of trying to convert the heathen managers to accept arbitrary alternatives that are at best of little value and at worst huge wastes of time.[1] To attract buyers, focus on the results that make the organization more successful and them more productive, and eschew the arbitrary and unfounded approaches that simply enrich the latest guru.

CREATING A "BRAND"

A "brand" is a recognition factor. That factor can be a name (McKinsey), a product (Coke), a concept (the old "dog/star," quadrant from Boston

---

[1]Even Abraham Maslow's famous "hierarchy of needs," a favorite metaphor for trainers and consultants all over the place, has *never* been validated as an accurate description of actual workplace behavior, motivations, or future responses. Maslow was a psychologist with fascinating ideas, but never worked as a consultant demonstrating his theory's utility to motivate and manage people. We have to be careful about what we preach to be true.

Consulting Group), a phrase ("engineered like no other car in the world"—Mercedes), or a promise ("absolutely, positively guaranteed to get there the next day"—FedEx).

Brands can be positive ("Get me Alan Weiss!") or negative ("Don't hire Arthur Andersen!"). They can convey lasting exemplary status (the Johnson & Johnson Tylenol crisis) and lasting obloquy (the *Exxon Valdez*). They become colloquialisms in the language ("Are you trying to be the Enron of the photography business?!"; "We are the Mercedes of the jewelry business.").

As I've tried to delicately point out along the way, human resources and internal consultants don't always have the best brand. In fact, they often have a negative brand. Fortunately, that's not fatal, because perceptions are fickle and can be readily managed. (That's why there's probably a public relations function in your organization and why that industry exists in general—to create positive images.)

The bottom line is that you will be branded in any case, *so why not take pains to try to ensure that the brand is positive and constructive?*

Perception is reality. Managing perception creates reality. Here are some tricks of the trade to create the best possible perception for yourself in the aftermath of success. None of this is based on falsity, manipulation, or dishonesty. It is simply based on consolidating and clarifying your success so that it is maximally understood and appreciated by prospective new clients. See Figure 10.4.

We establish in Chapter 1 that you require a market need, competency to fill that need, and passion to be truly successful as a consultant. Those three elements lead to your business positioning (either for you, personally, or your unit). That positioning may be as internal change agents, internal consultants, executive advisors, and so forth.

This is the point at which brands are established, when you want

---

The ultimate brand is your name. That's neither disloyal to the organization nor unfaithful to your colleagues. Just be sure to use your power for good works.

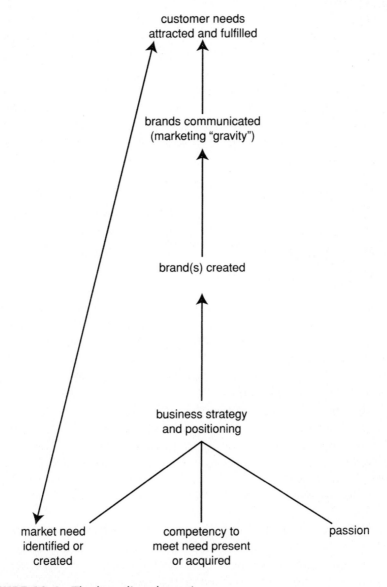

FIGURE 10.4 The branding dynamics

the client to say, "If we're going to have this off-site strategy meeting, then we need Gloria Jones to facilitate it, so make sure she's available." (That brand attraction contributes to marketing "gravity" which we discuss later in this chapter.)

The best and most singular brand is your name, because no one else can duplicate that and, most importantly, it eliminates external competitors. However, it takes time for your name to become the brand, so you are probably best served by developing interim brands. These may include phrases or competencies such as:

- ✔ The Change Makers.
- ✔ Facilitation Central.
- ✔ The Leadership Coaches.
- ✔ The Idea People.
- ✔ Trusted Advisors.
- ✔ The Change Masters.
- ✔ The Strategists.
- ✔ Conflict Busters.
- ✔ The Innovators.
- ✔ The Mediators.

I know this may sound overly cute, but I'm quite serious. You want to be *known* for something. The sales department has its "go to" people. The IT area has its top geeks. It's vital to overcome negative images of internal change agents to create positive spin, and you can best accomplish that when you have successful projects and ardent supporters in your recent history.

The strategy should follow the path in Figure 10.5. Isolate the strengths from the recent project(s),[2] establish your brand or brands based on those strengths, coordinate the dissemination, communicate consistently, and evolve as necessary (always aiming toward your name as the eventual brand).

As an example:

1. You've completed a highly successful project that created and merged career development (bottom up) with organizational succession planning needs (top down). You have several strong sponsors and a very happy buyer.
2. You establish a brand called Career Makers. And you create a catchphrase: "Don't let your job get in the way of your career,"

---

[2]You can use the Self-Development Template from this chapter.

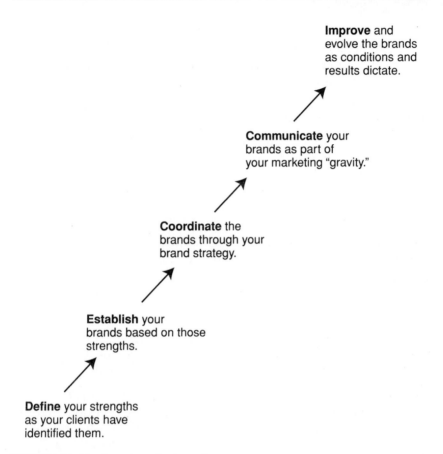

Improve and evolve the brands as conditions and results dictate.

Communicate your brands as part of your marketing "gravity."

Coordinate the brands through your brand strategy.

Establish your brands based on those strengths.

Define your strengths as your clients have identified them.

FIGURE 10.5 Creating the brand strategy

encouraging people to seek areas in which to utilize their talents aside from the traditional hierarchical ladder.

3. Your strategy for the brands is to attract both individual professionals seeking counseling and advice, and who might otherwise leave the organization in frustration at lack of advancement, creating a talent drain; and to attract senior division leaders who want to create more stable teams with bench strength and backup.

4. You write articles in the company publications using your brand and catchphrase. You put up posters on bulletin boards.

You establish a web site purely devoted to career development options. You initiate free lunchtime discussion on alternative career options. You meet privately for breakfast with division executives concerned about losing talent.

5. As more projects ensue, and more people come your way, you consider a publication, HR's Guide to Finding Your Route or even Alan's Ten Tips for Job Latitude on the web site. The executive morning meetings that you sponsor may become "Alan's meetings."

> I've seen sales teams called Rob's Rangers and customer service groups called Ann's Angels. These are terrific brands. Why can't you develop them as well?

Most internal consultants don't take marketing seriously and feel that branding is something that cereal companies do. But the path to a successful career—no matter how you choose to define it—is along the route of *perceived* competence, *perceived* assistance, and *perceived* results. The advantage of successful branding is that you don't have to prove yourself each and every time. The brand will speak for itself. In fact, there's probably a brand speaking for you right now. And the chances are that if you're not actively managing it, it ain't good.

MARKETING "GRAVITY"

I developed the concept of consulting marketing "gravity" in the mid-1990s when I realized the following:

✔ When prospective clients approach you (instead of your seeking them out) the entire psychological dynamic is changed. Rather than your needing to establish credibility and competence, the two of you are engaged in a joint decision about whether a relationship and partnership make sense.

✔ The resultant relationship is almost automatically at a peer level. A landscaper, plumber, or designer have far greater leverage when you seek their services on a referral basis rather than their approaching you and asking for business.

✔ It is far more cost effective and time effective.

✔ It's a lot less wearying.

Until I planned this book, I hadn't considered the ramifications for marketing gravity for internal consultants, but quickly realized that *it's even more important and more valuable for internal people.* The key barriers for internal change agents are lack of credibility, lack of visibility, lack of power, low position in the hierarchy, and perceptions of incompetence ("If we had good people internally we wouldn't have to look outside for help").

All of these reservations, real and imagined, are nullified by a strong "gravitational effect."

If you work hard to attract buyers to you, there will be far less work later. The interesting aspect of gravity is that it multiplies itself—as people are attracted to you, word spreads, and *more* people are attracted to you.

Not all aspects of an external consultant's marketing forces may apply, but because of the diversity of organizational life and the range of behaviors and risk taking among readers, I thought I'd present them all (Figure 10.6) and allow you to pick and choose. Not that I use the full range of the options described, so these aren't theoretical devices but rather highly pragmatic tactics.

I'll review these quickly, starting at 12 o'clock and working counterclockwise.

Pro Bono Work. Volunteer your efforts for the United Way campaign or a lunchtime series on the arts. Work elbow-to-elbow with se-

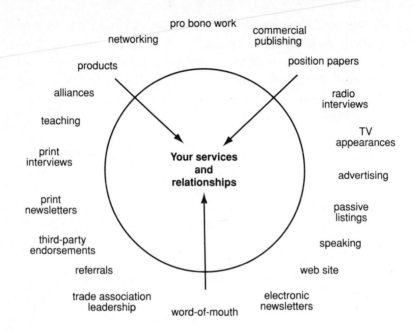

FIGURE 10.6 The elements of creating marketing gravity

nior people who have volunteered, and who can therefore observe your competency and enthusiasm in a collegial atmosphere.

Products. Produce job aids, pamphlets, and manuals that are innovative and proactive, not merely in response to requests. For example, if you note confusion about the organization's job posting mechanisms, create a flow chart explaining how to access options and at which times in the contribution process.

Alliances. Are there outside resources *that you can serve to manage and coordinate* and not compete with? Can you forge a relationship with a design firm or a software vendor? Note that one of the huge weaknesses of most organizations is that they do not know how to manage or coordinate multiple external consultants.

If no one ever seeks you out, you have no pull. Don't just sit by the phone bemoaning your fate (or, worse, talking about how stupid the management is). Do something to create some attraction. If you can't implement several of the alternatives provided here, you're in the wrong profession.

Teaching. Are you visible on the faculty of internal workshops and seminars? Best: Play a role in senior developmental programs on leadership, succession planning, competitive intelligence, and so on. Arrange to bring in an outside speaker on senior level topics whom you host and introduce.

Print Interviews. Suggest interviews within the company and outside it dealing with successful change strategies and contemporary issues.

Referrals. I've discussed the critical importance of gaining referrals from current buyers *while still engaged in their projects.*

Print and Electronic Newsletters. Create a weekly, monthly, and/or quarterly report, in hard copy or electronically, covering important organizational issues. You may choose to offer techniques on managing diverse employee groups or providing more responsive customer service, for example.

Third-Party Endorsements. If you've worked at other organizations in the past, or at different locations in the current organization, assemble a "best practices" portfolio of nonproprietary information that you can share with interested parties.

Trade Association Leadership. Your clients and prospects belong to outside trade associations, and so should you. Don't just be a silent member. Pursue a leadership role and the visibility and credentials that come with it. Become a thought leader and innovator in your field.

Word-of-Mouth. This will accrue naturally with your success, but help it along *by telling people what projects you're working on or have worked on.*

Web Site. If you don't have an appropriate corporate web site, think about creating one. Post your tips, newsletter, position papers, and other marketing materials on it.

Speaking. Similar to training, are you addressing company conferences on issues within your purview? Have you offered to do so? Are you being sought by external conferences and conventions to represent yourself and your company?

Passive Listings and Advertising. Perhaps not as appropriate internally, but how do buyers know that you're there and what your capabilities are? How are you listed in the company directory (e.g., as "HR" or as "consulting")? Are there bulletin boards and web sites you should be a part of to offer services? Is your Rolodex card on people's desktops?

Television and Radio Interviews. These may be tough but are not impossible. For example, Denny's has become famous for reversing its racist image and past and becoming a model for the best diversity and good business practices. Who was responsible internally? Company policy may prohibit such media involvement, but when it's in the name of positive image, it's usually encouraged.

Position Papers. Author papers about contemporary topics that can be downloaded or faxed to any part of the company. Topics could include: How to conduct a hiring interview that's effective and legal; How to provide feedback to a difficult employee; or How to ensure that individual objectives are aligned behind corporate goals.

Commercial Publishing. This, too, requires corporate permission in many cases, but many people have done it. Demonstrate your competence through magazines, newspapers, newsletters, and web sites that value your opinions, methodology, and experiences. If it's good enough to share with outsiders, it must be good enough for your own colleagues, right?

As you progress in your consulting career, more and more people should be attracted to you if you've created the proper gravity. (See Figure 10.7.)

In the aftermath of successful projects, your marketing gravity should be exponentially intensifying. It can be lethal not to have any successful projects, but it's absolutely negligent to have them and bury them without fanfare or leverage. You may be a consultant like me, but you're also, like me, in the marketing business.

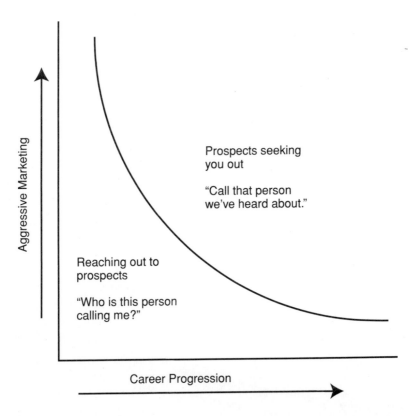

Prospects seeking you out

"Call that person we've heard about."

Reaching out to prospects

"Who is this person calling me?"

Aggressive Marketing

Career Progression

FIGURE 10.7 Moving toward greater attraction

SUGGESTED READING

Danger in the Comfort Zone, by Judith Bardwick (amacom, 1991). This is one of my favorite business books, with a subtitle that includes the phrase "How to break the entitlement habit." It's useful for your prospects but also useful as a self-examination of your own role and philosophy. The perfect world is not zero stress, but enough stress to create a sense of urgency and jolt us out of our comfort zone, which the marketing gravity approach may require of you.

11

The Ethical Quandaries

When to Put Up, Shut Up, and Give Up

THE ETHICAL TEMPLATE

Consulting has traditionally been on the front line of organizational ethics. The Enron/Andersen debacle has simply accentuated a factor that most of us seriously involved in the profession had long known: You don't consult successfully unless you are clear about ethical imperatives—both your own and the clients'.

This is both easier and harder for the internal consultant. Easier, because you are able to view ethical behavior or suspected misbehavior in context over time. Harder, because confronting it can easily mean confronting your own future and career.

This is an area in which I find a clear template highly useful. The one I choose to use looks like Figure 11.1.

Both you and your organization require three conditions in order to act ethically:

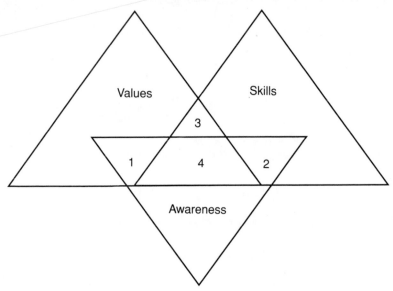

1. "Would act" but can't, because of lack of skills.
2. "Should act" but won't, because of lack of values.
3. "Could act" but doesn't, because of lack of awareness.
4. "Will act" because all elements are present.

FIGURE 11.1   The ethical template

1. *Values* are the elements of your belief system that tell you something is "right" or "wrong." Some organizations (GE, for example) clearly state and enforce the values that managers must meet performance goals but also must meet them in the right way. Others (multilevel sales networking schemes) clearly believe that it's important to bring in new members, irrespective of whether they'll be able to ever make money themselves in the pyramid.

2. *Skills* are the competencies and knowledge required to do something about an ethical transgression. If you can't cite company policy, can't confront misbehavior, and can't stand up to a bully, you don't have the armament to do ethical battle.

3. *Awareness* is the environmental sensitivity about what's going on. All the values and skills in the world are meaningless if you're unaware of the harassment next door or discriminatory hiring practices upstairs.

There are, of course, ethical gray areas that require analysis and even introspection. But they are the minority. Most matters of right and wrong are clear. It's important to remember that what is legal might not always be ethical, and what is unethical might not always be illegal. That's why ethics should be in the purview of internal consultants and not the legal department.

The reason the template is so useful is that you can objectively measure your organization's (and your own) preparedness to face ethical challenges. All three elements must be present. Many managers were aware of overt racism in the old Denny's organization, or in Texaco at one well-documented period, and they could have dealt with it if they had chosen. But the prevailing value system at the time stipulated that nothing was wrong with it.

Organizations don't suddenly become unethical, nor do leaders gather to decide how to skirt the moral boundaries. In the case study on page 218, what actually occurred was a phenomenon I call "the thermal zone." This is a refractory area, not unlike a warm layer of ocean water, which changes and distorts sound and light. It occurs when middle management acts in its own self-interest and no one bothers to try to align goals behind corporate direction.

It is inevitably a surprise to senior leadership when they encounter the adverse results, completely discordant with their intentions. (See Figure 11.2.)

One of the most valuable roles internal consultants can play, therefore, is to ensure that the objectives, monitoring, and evaluation of all managers down the line are consistent with corporate direction and support those goals.

Case Study

I had been hired to do a baseline study of diversity at a Fortune 25 organization. While conducting the focus groups, interviews, observations, and surveys, I found institutionalized discrimination, not from malice so much as from ignorance and terrible biases.

Asians were believed to be incapable of managing. African-Americans were believed to be spreading rumors whenever they were seen talking among themselves; people with accents, for whom English was a second language, were not promoted as frequently as native English speakers; the seating patterns in the cafeteria suggested tribal villages more than a mosaic, much less an integrated whole.

My report was passed like a hot potato to the CEO, who burst out, "This is not my company! This is simply not true!"

His values were fine, as were his skills. But he had no awareness at all of day-to-day corporate reality. To his credit, he calmed down, demanded changes, and personally held his senior people accountable for changing beliefs and behaviors.

Of course, this demands that:

- ✔ You are aware of the corporate goals.
- ✔ You communicate the corporate goals.
- ✔ You work with key managers to create consistent performance objectives.
- ✔ You possess the three elements of ethics to support and enforce those goals.

The advantage of the internal consultant is in being able to see, evaluate, and help change behavior every day. When an outside consultant is brought in for an "ethics audit" or "ethics training" or some such thing, you know that internal people have failed. Ethics don't

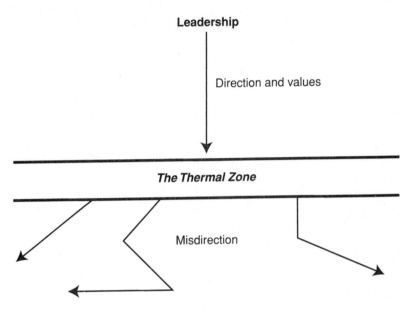

FIGURE 11.2 The Thermal Zone

Passivity is the same as endorsement of unethical acts. If you're not opposed to them, then you are supporting them. There is no neutrality in ethics. "Oh, that's the sales force," or "Boys will be boys," or "No harm, no foul," are dangerous platitudes. If you can't be an ethical exemplar, then get out of the way.

constitute a project or a procedure, but rather are part of the fabric of corporate life.

This means that before, during, after, amid, and alongside your project work, ethical considerations should be preeminent, just as would be safety, legality, and civility. These are aspects of our corporate life, and not independent variables.

Any suspected or presumed transgression can be objectively dealt with if the management is adept with the template:

Is something occurring that is questionable?

What do my values tell me is the right thing to do?

What skills are required to resolve the issue?

The same applies to any internal consultant who may be thrust into roiling waters. The buyer isn't always right. That being the case, what can you do about it?

Case Study

I was in a senior level meeting about the need to cut costs during an industry recession when the internal consultant assigned to the project began talking about "attrits." I had no idea what "attrits" were, and assumed them to be part of the firm's technical jargon.

As I listened to her go into "three levels of diminishing severance," however, I was horrified to discover that she was talking about deliberate attrition—layoffs en masse—and that the victims of this devastation had been short-handed to "attrits" in her lexicon.

When I was able to get my buyer aside later, I told him that if his internal people were going to be so callous and unethical, then the plan was doomed and, most probably, so was he. I suggested a more rational approach to intelligent cost reduction, and the abandonment of all such impersonal language immediately.

The internal person was dropped like a hot potato. She was basically a nice woman, and I had the opportunity to later ask why she had chosen that route.

"It's the way the client approached me," she explained. "I thought I was giving him what he wanted."

Precisely. What he wanted was wrong and that's what consultants must point out. He changed his mind rapidly enough, once confronted.

BLOWING THE WHISTLE

For an extended period in the 1990s, Astra Pharmaceuticals, head-quartered in Massachusetts in the United States but owned by a Swedish parent, was the scene of egregious sexual harassment emanating from the then-president and many top managers. This was documented in court filings and resulted in terminations, lawsuits, convictions, and settlements.

Those activities were well-known, it turned out, within the company, but no one was willing to come forward, to blow the whistle, to oppose the practices,[1] until one brave victimized woman sounded the alarm. Where was Human Resources? No one seems to know, although in the aftermath the U.S. HR head left the company, replaced by an attorney as vice president.

When I posed the Astra conundrum to 10 retired executive vice presidents of human resources during an interview session, 7 of them refused to comment or condemn what had happened at Astra because "we weren't there," "we don't have all the facts," and, my favorite, "I'm not familiar with the incident" (which was merely the cover story of most major news magazines and newspapers, not to mention broadcast media and the Internet).

How was racism allowed to reach clichéd proportions at Texaco? Who advised the CEO of Exxon to be unavailable for 48 hours immediately following the *Exxon Valdez* tragedy? Why was Bob Allen, then CEO of AT&T, not dissuaded from announcing the intended layoffs of 40,000 people, mostly to atone for his own strategic blunders, such as a $325 million loss in an ill-advised foray into computers?[2]

Internal consultants must be willing to cry "Foul!" There's a difference between being the horribly, stereotypical, bureaucratic traffic cop who stalls initiatives, seeks reasons for change *not* to occur, and plays "gotcha"; and in being an objective voice of ethical fair play, defender of individual dignity, and sought-out counselor. There is a rea-

---

[1]And some of those practices included parties where sexual favors were expected. The president was quoted as telling employees, "You have 24 hours in a day—8 to work, 8 to play, and 8 to sleep."

[2]Allen's move was so repugnant that public pressure finally stopped the terminations.

> If there are no referees blowing the whistle, then the team that most ignores the rules, most acts like a bully, and most hurts the opposition will win. The only side to be on is the *right* side, even if that means you're a team of one.

son for senior executives making horribly bad decisions, ignoring ethical boundaries, and endangering their organizations: No one internally is stopping them. Edmund Burke said that "The only thing necessary for the triumph of evil is for good men to do nothing."

In ethical quagmires, internal consultants must do something.

Case Study

An organization in the top 50 of the Fortune 500 had acquired a multibillion dollar company. The executive vice president, Ralph, son of the original founder, was a tyrant. He routinely screamed at people, used horrible obscenities at meetings, and generally brutalized even peers. People tried to keep out of his gun sights.

The president of the new subsidiary asked me to help build a team spirit more in line with the parent, well-known for its stellar workplace. I told him that Ralph must go. The president told me that Ralph simply "had a style" that people "understood."

We compromised on a 360° review, which, under promises of anonymity, was finally eliciting how people really felt about Ralph. Midway through, however, Ralph decided that he needed his own consultant, and lobbied to have someone brought in from far away to run the assessment.

The president agreed and I happily left. It was time to get out of the morass. No one else blew the whistle and, when I did, no one wanted to hear it. The last I heard, Ralph was still there, as dysfunctional as ever.

Fortunately, there is a variety of ways in which to blow the whistle. Here is an escalating scale.

1. Discussions with the performer. Gather evidence and observed behavior and provide the performer with the benefit of the doubt. "Are you aware that when you ask for questions after the management meetings, you never recognize women with their hands in the air?" "People in your division, and I, have watched you remove computer equipment from the office. It's creating a question about what you're doing with it, and I thought we could avoid rumors by clarifying the situation." The actions may be inadvertent, innocent, or explicable, so give the person the opportunity to recognize, explain, and/or rectify.

Most ethical transgressions are committed on behalf of the organization, not for individual gain. That makes them no less serious and can, in fact, create peer pressure to engage in the same acts in a sense of distorted loyalty.

2. Confrontation with the performer. If you have unequivocal evidence and the performer denies it or refuses to do anything about it, you must demand change. "You are turning in repair confirmations that are not signed by the customer, despite prior warnings. We have proof from the customers themselves. If you don't take the time to ensure they're pleased and have them sign off on the work, you will be reported to your superior." If you make a threat, you must be prepared to carry through with it, or you will merely enable the behavior still further.

3. Report the situation to management and monitor action. If a manager has been reported using racist language at meetings, and that person denies it or refuses to stop, report the individual to the immediate superior with recommendations for

action (e.g., suspension, re-education, apologies, termination, etc.). If management does not enforce any disciplinary measures *immediately*, proceed to the next level of management. Continue this until someone does take action, *not only on the offender but also on the offender's management who refused to take action.*

4. Proceed to other organizational sources. If local management refuses to take action, go to the legal department, the corporate ombudsman, the parent, senior management from an-

---

Case Study

A woman who had known me from my work in her prior organization called me and asked for advice. She told me that she had been dating the president of her new employer (both were divorced) and had moved in with him.

One day he informed her that the relationship was over, threw her out of his house, and encouraged her to resign. When she refused to leave the company, he arranged for increasingly odious assignments and denied her any increases and opportunities for improved circumstances. No one internally was willing to confront the president, so she was isolated and actually encouraged by human resources to leave with a modest severance package.

I told her to contact the executive vice president of the parent company—a major insurer with a carefully-honed reputation—and explain in detail what had happened. She was to tell him that she trusted him to resolve the situation, but if he didn't, she'd be forced to seek external relief.

Within seven days of fact-finding, the executive vice president fired the president of the subsidiary, and offered the woman a better job or a generous severance package, whichever she preferred. She accepted the latter.

Would the outcome have been any different if an internal consultant had provided the same assistance I had? I doubt it.

other department, or any other internal source that may intervene. Remember that if you simply give up, no matter how hard you previously tried, you have now become complicit in perpetuating the unethical behavior.

5. Alert external agencies. If necessary, contact the police, regulatory authorities, support groups, trade associations, your congressional representative, or whoever might be of help and would have the means and interest to intervene. Might this mean that your career there is over? Perhaps you might have to leave the morass, or perhaps you'll become a hero. Either possibility is better than the alternative of doing nothing if the transgression is serious.

6. Alert the media. This is the ultimate and most dramatic form of whistle-blowing, and it's too often used prior to any steps listed earlier. It's the last resort, rarely needed, and impossible to retract, but its mere threat is often sufficient to create action.

Might taking a stand effectively end your career? Only if you look at your career as a static thing rooted in that organization and culture. Your career—and your life—is larger than that. Ironically, your career can be blunted, ruined, and sullied by *not* taking a stand.

In my experience, consultants become involved in ethical imbroglios much more frequently today than ever before. If you want to be conservative but firm in your resistance to unethical acts, then use these criteria:

✔ Move up the scale of interventions; don't jump to the more dramatic and public responses if you haven't considered the more intimate and private ones.

✔ Use only observed behavior and objective evidence. Do not operate on hearsay or rumor. Someone claiming ill treatment or harassment is only a claimant, not a victim, until evidence is found.

✔ Use Occam's razor (the most probable solution is usually the simplest) as your philosophy. Miscommunication, ignorance of policy, and poor judgment are more likely causes than malice and deliberate misbehavior most of the time.

✔ Hear both sides of the story. Unpopular people are often falsely accused.

✔ If you make a threat, intend to carry it out if needed.

✔ Don't pursue trivialities with equal fervor. Judgment is essential. Cheating on an expense report is more serious than taking home a pencil from one's desk.

Decide whether the issue is one that requires a fight to the death, or if you'd be better off living to fight another day.

LIVING TO FIGHT ANOTHER DAY

I was always fascinated by the historical comparison that the Greeks believed nothing was more glorious than to die in battle, and the Romans believed that prudence was important, because you could always win back tomorrow what you lost today. Lives were considered important to preserve.

The Romans had the far more successful and long-lived civilization.

Not all transgressions require falling on your sword. I realize that you may be thinking "There's no such thing as being a little pregnant," but ethics don't quite possess that same degree of clear biological determinism. Here are some minitests that you should quickly consider to determine in each one the following:

✔ Ignore: Minor or unimportant, or not really an ethical matter.

✔ Resist: You personally abjure and insist others should resist, but it's not a career-on-the-line issue.

✔ Fight: You demand change, escalating up the sequence above, and you are willing to be fired if that's what it takes. If you get no relief, you voluntarily leave.

> "In matters of taste, swim with the tide; in matters of principle, stand like a rock."—Thomas Jefferson

Case 1 In the course of your succession planning project, you hear the buyer say to his sales vice president, "Any women who have high potential shift over to other parts of the business where they stand a decent chance. They'll never make it in our sales arena, and we owe them a better shot than that."

Case 2 While walking through a remote warehouse, you see an old-fashioned pinup calendar with scantily clad women. Only three men work in the warehouse three days a week.

Case 3 Employees are using phones for personal calls, and sometimes using the computers to receive private e-mails.

Case 4 In working on a customer satisfaction survey, you learn that the salespeople are often using hyperbole to sell the product ("This widget is far better than even more expensive models") and promising questionable things ("We generally can't deliver that quickly, but I'll check with distribution to see if it's possible to send these within 48 hours").

Case 5 Delivering workshops on an unrelated issue, you hear several employees encouraging others not to participate in the charitable drive organized by the company because they don't approve of the political position of the charity receiving the donations.

Case 6 Working on an expense reduction assignment, you find senior managers frequently buying expensive meals for each other and claiming "customer entertainment" on their expense reports. Company policy specifically forbids meals to be expenses, even if business is discussed during them.

Case 7 A hiring manager scans resumes only for a minute, looking for a key word or work experience, before discarding them, despite the money invested in the ad campaign and quality hiring initiative you're working on.

Case 8 A vice president returns his first class airplane tickets—to which he is entitled—for coach tickets, and either pockets the difference or uses it for his wife's expenses to accompany him.

Case 9 Because it's important to move rapidly on a project, the buyer tells you to proceed before she has received permission to expend the funds. She tells you it's her responsibility and to charge ahead.

Case 10 A candidate for a job shows up with confidential, competitive information that could immensely help your sales and undermine that competitor. Of the four of you on the hiring team, the three others agree it should be accepted and read, including the senior vice president of marketing.

Responses: There are, perhaps, no right answers, since these are brief and sterile examples without much context. But they are all taken from actual incidents, and I contend that the following alternatives are probably best:

Case 1 Fight. Discrimination with good intentions is as bad as discrimination with malicious intentions. It's still discrimination.

Case 2 Fight. This creates a hostile work environment, even if that's not the case for the guys who normally work there. You now know it's there, and it must be removed.

Case 3 Resist. You may frown on this, depending on company policy (many organizations allow reasonable usage, which actually improves productivity) but this is common practice and does virtually no harm.

Case 4   Ignore. As long as no one is lying about the product or covering up deficiencies, it's safe to be even overly enthusiastic. Customers expect salespeople to be biased supporters of their own wares.[3]

Case 5   Ignore. This is clearly free speech and it's not your job to lobby on behalf of the company's chosen charity.

Case 6   Resist. This is a clear ethical violation, and you should raise it and condemn it. (The amounts don't matter—in for a dime, in for a dollar.) However, you're probably not wise to put your job on the line against a relatively minor problem (the net expense cost of such things is tiny).

Case 7   Ignore. That's at his or her discretion, and maybe the system works for that person. You might want to show them a more effective means, if you have one, but there's nothing unethical about the speed.

Case 8   Fight. This is theft, and it sets an example of theft. Even though entitled to the comfort of first class, the company has not said that the person is entitled to the cash equivalent of first class. (Otherwise, why not trade in the computer or cell phone for cheaper equipment and keep the difference?) I've seen widespread thievery result from these bad examples.

> You can ignore, resist, or fight. Choose your battles. Remember, if you're serious, you can probably afford to lose only one fight. But if it's the right one, you can leave with your head high, knowing that it would be even worse to stay.

[3]There are exceptions. In the pharmaceutical industry, for example, "fair balance" is essential, to the extent that salespeople must disclose such things as adverse side effects even if unasked.

Case 9   Ignore. She's the buyer, it's her accountability, and she admits it. You might want to get your marching orders in writing, but there's nothing here for you to resist.

Case 10   Fight. This is absolutely inappropriate, because it fails the "reversal test": If it were our company on the other end, would we accept this as fair play? It also fails the "stink test": If this episode were printed in the *Wall Street Journal* tomorrow, would we be proud or would be need to take a shower? Stealing through an offer is no better than stealing by breaking and entering.

In the course of your consulting assignments, it really doesn't matter whether the ethical problems you discover are germane to the project or not. What matters is that they are relevant to the organization that you represent. There is no such thing as an irrelevant ethical issue.

It also may seem frighteningly vague to consider that there are varying responses according to the severity. But this is an increasingly complex age. Nationwide, about half of all marriages end in divorce. About 40 percent of all children are born out of wedlock. Same-sex relationships often qualify for company benefit plans. Instantaneous messaging precludes the thoughtfulness and scrutiny we would often give to our communications, and sometimes sends information into unintended hands. Television now broadcasts graphic nudity, violence, and obscenity.

Mores, beliefs, and standards continue to change. There are behaviors that are clearly right and wrong, and still others that necessitate analysis. My own criteria have usually included these guidelines:

- ✔ When harm is deliberately being done to others,[4] fight, with the intention of removing the malefactors.
- ✔ When harm is inadvertently being done to others, fight, with the intention of educating the transgressors.

---

[4]"Others" includes employees, vendors, customers, colleagues, and any other stakeholders or affected parties.

Sometimes, you fight and lose. Or you despair at the magnitude of what must be fought. In such cases, it may just be time to go.

WHEN IT'S TIME TO GO

One of the greatest types of leverage for an external consultant (or any services provider) is to be willing to walk away from business. Often, the client calls you back and says, "Wait, don't go; we'll find the money." Sometimes the buyer allows you to leave, meaning that you've avoided bad business.

For an internal consultant, walking away from business may mean walking away from your job. But that's the way it should be.

> No one should spend a career in human resources, uninterrupted by stints in the real trenches of business. You can't depend on layoffs and downsizings. Sometimes, you have to fire your employer.

I read a letter to the editor of a magazine recently from someone who proclaimed he had spent the past 40 years in Human Resources. My reaction was to dismiss his comments. What on earth could he possibly know about business? (Another letter, one of my favorites, was from a woman protesting that there were too many ads in *Training* magazine, thereby vividly portraying the total disconnectedness of her perspective with business. Was the magazine to finance its operation through bake sales?)

A group of retired human resources executives informed me during a group discussion that they were "tired of the issue about a 'seat at the table,' " and that it was no longer a subject for discussion. It was no longer a subject for discussion, I suspect, because none of them had figured out how to assume a peer position at the top of the organization, not because it was being done so often.

If you truly want to be an effective internal change agent, then ideally you must possess the following:

Skills	*Traits*	*Experiences*
✔ Frame issues quickly.	✔ High assertiveness.	✔ Line management.
✔ Resolve conflict rapidly.	✔ High persuasiveness.	✔ P&L responsibility.
✔ Communicate effectively.	✔ High energy level.	✔ Sales and/or marketing.
✔ Counseling/ coaching.	✔ Innovation/ creativity.	✔ Turn-around poor operation.
✔ Marketing/ promotion.	✔ Ethics/ integrity.	✔ International travel.
✔ Work well in ambiguity.	✔ Approachability.	✔ Basic technical usage.
✔ Rapid problem solving.	✔ Deductive reasoning.	✔ Client interaction.
✔ Risk analysis.	✔ Prudent risk taking.	✔ Team leadership.
✔ Financial analysis.	✔ Flexibility.	✔ Valuable failures.[5]
✔ Strategic planning.	✔ Big picture thinker.	✔ Work with diverse people.

The likelihood of this combination of skills, traits, and experiences taking place within one company (and within a reasonable time frame) is miniscule. Winston Churchill said, "We build our houses, and then they shape us." Spending too much time in any one organization actually stunts growth and narrows perspective *no matter how excellent that organization may be*, and there are precious few excellent organizations.

The ability of an external consultant to garner the characteristics just listed from a diversity of assignments is not difficult. I advise even external people to have held down some honest jobs along the way, so that the line management experience and customer interactions are satisfied.

For internal people, walking away is not just a *reactive* move from poor conditions, but also a *proactive* move to seek still better (or just differing) conditions.

---

[5] We don't learn unless we fail, and it's good to fail on someone else's dime, if possible.

There are few things more pathetic than the 35-year veteran HR vice president who does whatever the CEO instructs, appears to perform his or her tap dance at certain corporate events, and is otherwise most concerned about not rocking the boat. Internal consultants should be making waves and sometimes turning the boat over.

Here is when it's time to go. When internal people are downsized, it's usually because they've missed or ignored the signs that it was time to go all along the way.

Reactive Signs

- ✔ No one is calling for your help, no matter how much you promote it, because personal agendas and politics take precedence over productivity and performance.
- ✔ You are constantly unable to work with department, division, and functional heads, and must deal with lower-level people who cannot commit to agreements nor provide resources.
- ✔ The organization is in flux, you are shuffled around, and/or you find yourself reporting to legal, administrative services, or other generic catch-alls instead of a true internal consulting function.
- ✔ You've become a pair of hands called in like a plumber or electrician. That is, you don't participate in the "what" and "why" discussions for an intervention or project, but are merely told "how" to get something done for someone and are expected to execute.
- ✔ Your pay grade, status, and overall perception of others place you in an inferior position to organizational managers.
- ✔ Despite your past successes and proclaimed competence, external consultants are hired for any major project and you are either not considered or relegated to minor support roles.
- ✔ Arbitrary layoffs are instituted.

Proactive Signs

✔ You are not learning or growing, and what you do well you can do in your sleep. There is no challenge.

✔ You realize there are key elements missing in your development that are unlikely to be filled in the near future if you don't make a move.[6]

✔ Your analysis of the profession, environment, and/or community tells you that others in your position are being treated better, utilized better, and paid better elsewhere.

✔ You dislike the people and/or values around you.

If you want to be a change agent, then don't be hesitant about changing your own life and your own career. Keep testing the envelope. I've never heard any buyer, anywhere, state, "Get me the most conservative consultant you can! We want to make only fine adjustments!" Buyers want real change. If we can't change ourselves, how can we help others to change?

Whatever you do, don't hold onto a job merely because it's paying the bills. The best external consultants are as good as they are because they are accustomed to risk, seldom have the opportunity to play it safe, and have no guaranteed weekly paycheck or security, other than what they produce. When you cling to a position that is no longer challenging, or is degrading, or is part of an unethical organization, you not only continue to enable its behavior but you erode your own behavior.

---

[6]This is why my chart is useful, even if you change it to better customize it for your needs. If you don't have a list of ingredients for your future, how do you know if the current food is nutritional?

Consulting is that rare profession in which we're paid to learn, which increases our value, which means that the next client will pay us still more to learn still more, which will enhance our value still more. With such a rare opportunity facing us, it's criminal not to take advantage of the opportunities of consulting.

Become your own best client, and heed your own best advice.

SUGGESTED READING

The Doom Loop System, by Dory Hollander, Ph.D. (Viking, 1991). Although it uses the ubiquitous quadrants, this is a fine career management work, looking at experience and environment to determine when it's time to go (or how to make it better to stay).

— More Suggested Readings —

Argyris, Chris. *Integrating the Individual and the Organization*. Wiley & Sons, 1964.

    A prolific writer and preeminent psychologist; this is his work on combining positive team building with individual well-being to create improved performance.

Bellman, Geoffrey. *The Consultant's Calling*. Jossey-Bass, 1990.

    One of the philosophic books on consulting you should read. Geoff focuses on the philosophy and values of the profession.

Bennis, Warren and Burt Nanus. *The Unconscious Conspiracy*. amacom, 1976.

    The original and still best work by Bennis on leadership, subtitled, *Why Leaders Can't Lead*. Everything else he's done is really a variation of this work's. "Leaders are made" philosophy.

Drucker, Peter. *The Changing World of the Executive*. Times Books, 1982.

    One of the master's two best, the other being *The Effective Executive*.

———. *The Effective Executive*. Harper & Row, 1966.

    The only person who makes my list twice. This is still a powerful work, and probably his best.

Fiedler, Frederick. *A Theory of Leadership Effectiveness*. McGraw-Hill, 1967.

    The champion, perhaps, of the contingency theory approach to leadership.

Gabor, Andrea. *The Capitalist Philosophers.* Times Business, 2000.
> An extraordinary set of brief biographies, from Mary Parker Follet to Elton Mayo and Peter Drucker. This has been required reading in my graduate classes.

Gardner, John. *On Leadership.* Free Press, 1990.
> Simply one of the best, most succinct writers on the subject.

Gibson, James, et al. *Organizations.* BPI/Irwin, 1988.
> A graduate-level, excellent text. Later versions are probably available.

Gilbert, Tom. *Human Competence.* McGraw-Hill, 1978.
> Work carried on by Geary Rummler today. Focus on the performer as part of a stimulus-response dynamic.

Jay, Antony. *Management and Machiavelli.* Bantam, 1967.
> Enjoyable and lucid discussion of politics and maneuvering in organizational cultures.

Likert, Rensis. *New Patterns of Management.* McGraw-Hill, 1970.
> One of the toughest writers to comprehend; nevertheless his studies on leadership and performance led to some groundbreaking work at the University of Michigan.

Mager, Robert. *The Mager Library.* Pittman Learning, 1984.
> If you haven't read the collected—and insightfully funny— works of Mager, you aren't educated in this industry.

Maslow, Abraham. *Motivation and Personality.* Harper & Row, 1970.
> Classic work on hierarchy of needs and human motivation.

McClelland, David. *Human Motivation.* Scott, Foresman, 1985.
> Need/achievement theory and connections to Maslow's work.

McGregor, David. *The Human Side of Enterprise. McGraw-Hill, 1960.*
> His classic work on Theory X and Theory Y.

Sampson, Anthony. *The Company Man*. Times Business, 1995.
    A good history of companies, organizations, and the reasons for their current structure.

Schein, Edgar. *Process Consultation*. Addison-Wesley, 1969.
    Still *the* authority on process consultation.

Schultz, Duane and Sydney Ellen Schultz. *Psychology and Industry Today*. Macmillan, 1990.
    A graduate-level text that's clear and coherent. This is the fifth edition, and there is probably a newer one available.

Taylor, Frederick Winslow. *Scientific Management*. Harper, 1911.
    This is a terrific book, by the "first" management consultant. A "must" read if you're serious about the profession.

Vroom, Victor and Philip Yetton. *Leadership and Decision Making*. University of Pittsburgh Press, 1973.
    More recent work is available, but this is their seminal book on situational leadership. It's tough sledding. Often referred to as "normative" or "path/goal" theory.

Weiss, Alan. *Million Dollar Consulting: The Professional's Guide to Building A Practice*. McGraw-Hill, 1992, 1998, 2002.
    Still my best seller after all these years.

Zaleznik, Abraham. *The Managerial Mystique*. Harper & Row, 1989.
    One of the most vocal in terms of "leaders are born, not made." A counterpoint to the work of Bennis.

Index

About the Author

Alan Weiss began his own consulting firm, Summit Consulting Group, Inc., out of his home in 1985 after being fired by a boss with whom he shared a mutual antipathy. Today he still works out of his home, having traveled to 51 countries and 49 states, published 21 books and more than 500 articles, and consulted with some of the great organizations in the world, developing a seven-figure practice in the process.

His clients have included Merck, Hewlett-Packard, Federal Reserve Bank, State Street Corporation, Fleet Bank, Coldwell Banker, Textron, American Press Institute, Chase, Mercedes-Benz, GE, American Institute of Architects, British Standards Institute, and more than 300 similar organizations. He delivers 50 keynote speeches a year and is one of the stars of the lecture circuit. He appears frequently in the media to discuss issues pertaining to productivity and performance, and has been featured in teleconferences, videoconferences, and Internet conferences.

His Ph.D. is in organizational psychology, and he has served as a visiting faculty member at Case Western Reserve, St. John's, Tufts, and a half dozen other major universities. He currently holds an appointment as adjunct professor at the graduate school of business at the University of Rhode Island, where he teaches a highly popular course on advanced consulting skills. His books have been translated into German, Italian, and Chinese.

The *New York Post* has called him "one of the most highly respected independent consultants in the country," and *Success Magazine*, in an editorial devoted to his work, cited him as "a worldwide expert in executive education." His friends call him "the rock star of consulting."

Dr. Weiss resides with his wife of 34 years, Maria, in East Greenwich, Rhode Island with their dogs Phoebe and Koufax.